THE YIDDISH
SONG BOOK

SAW MILL MUSIC CORP.
160 High Street
Hastings On Hudson, NY 10706
(914) 478-2651

THE YIDDISH SONG BOOK

JERRY SILVERMAN

5B

A SCARBOROUGH BOOK
STEIN AND DAY/Publishers
Scarborough House, Briarcliff Manor, N.Y. 10510

ACKNOWLEDGMENTS

The following songs are included in this collection with the permission of the copyright holder, The Workman's Circle. They are all by Mordecai Gebirtig:

"Moyshele, Mayn Fraynd"
"Lidi fun Goldenem Land"
"Es Brent"

In addition, the following public-domain songs appear in the Workman's Circle publication *Mir Trogn a Gezang*, by Eleanor Gordon Mlotek, my source for them:

"Fun Vanen Heybt Zich On a Libe"
"A Cholem"
"In der Kuznye"
"Shprayz Ich Mir"
"Di Bord"
"Hirsh Lekert"
"Kishenever Pogrom"

First published in 1983
Copyright © 1983 by Jerry Silverman
All rights reserved.
Designed by Louis A. Ditizio
Printed in the United States of America
STEIN AND DAY/*Publishers*
Scarborough House
Briarcliff Manor, N.Y. 10510

Library of Congress Cataloging in Publication Data

Main entry under title:
  The Yiddish songbook.
  Unacc. melodies with chord symbols.
  Words in English and Yiddish (romanized)
  1. Jews—Music. 2. Music. 3. Folk-songs,
Yiddish. 4. Songs, Yiddish. I. Silverman,
Jerry.
M1852.Y5   1983   81-40331
ISBN 0-8128-2829-1
ISBN 0-8128-6130-2 (pbk.)

The Yiddish folk songs, why they are the most sincere, the most heartfelt I have heard anywhere. They are the truest expression of the soul of a people.

Albert Einstein

FORSHPAYS

Yiddish has always been a family affair.

In the Old Country you spoke Russian or Polish or Hungarian or Rumanian or Lithuanian or whatever on the "outside"—but when you came home and closed the door, it was *mame loshn*, the mother tongue.

Then came the great exodus—greater than in biblical times, the Diaspora raised to the nth degree. As the thousands passed through Ellis Island they carried their *yiddishkayt* with them in their wicker baskets and battered valises. But slowly the *yiddishkayt* began slipping away. The children of the immigrants of the 1880s and 1890s were the doughboys in France in World War I. The children of the immigrants of the teens and the twenties stood on the breadlines of the Depression and later were the GIs who liberated Buchenwald. *Yiddishkayt* stopped there. What sixty years of emigration was slowly eroding came to a terrible, nightmarish, inconceivable end in just six short years. The fountain was cut off at its source. And yet, and yet . . .

The wellspring of *yiddishkayt* runs deep. Maybe the mainstream was dried up, but the tributaries remain.

Consider this: my mother, Helen, who came to America from the *shtetl* of Dubrovno in Byelorussia as a teenager in 1913, and my son David, who was born in New York City fifty-six years later, both contributed directly to the writing of this book.

My mother's contribution consisted of her familiarity with much of the material itself and her knowledge of Yiddish as well as her willingness, her eagerness to find just the right word or shade of interpretation in the translations. My son's contribution was unique and, in a way, touching, for he, at the age of eleven, in his fourth year of studies at the Westchester Childrens' *Shul* in New York, was able to look up Yiddish words in the Yiddish-English dictionary—something that his father, who learned Yiddish by ear, was not able to do until recently.

The circle is unbroken. Yiddish has always been a family affair—an extended family affair, as well.

Consider this: Pauline Herman left her *shtetl* of Glubokoye (or, as the Jews called it, Gliboke) for America as a teenager in 1921. Glubokoye is about two hundred kilometers to the northwest of Dubrovno, not far from Vilna. Eventually marrying and settling in the Bronx, she and her husband ran a kosher delicatessen on the corner of Allerton Avenue and White Plains Road for many years. By the early 1960s the face of the old neighborhood had undergone a dramatic change as new waves of immigrants from different lands began moving in at an ever-increasing tempo. Tastes change—*de gustibus non disputandum est*— the old deli is now a doughnut shop.

That neighborhood was my childhood neighborhood, too. Several moves and half a lifetime later, the grandchildren of the one-time *Gliboker maydele* are schoolmates and playmates of the grandchildren of the *Dubrovner maydele*. Our famlies are closely tied by many bonds, tangible and intangible. Pauline, too, knows the songs, knows Yiddish (to be sure), and willingly helps with some points of translation as well as in the contribution of a modern Yiddish-American song, "*To Gey Zich Lernen Tantsn*."

Another link in the chain is Halina Rubinstein. Her mother, Leah, emigrated from Zhelechov (seventy-five kilometers from Warsaw) to Mexico in the 1920s. Halina studied, and later taught, Yiddish in the Yiddish *shul* in Mexico City. In 1970 she moved to the United States with her husband, Boris. What happened next? Simple! The granddaughter of the *Zhelechover maydele* found herself in the same class as one of the grandsons of the *Dubrovner maydele*—another intersection of orbits. Halina supplied the transliteration of several Yiddish texts. The ways of the folk process are mysterious and amazing!

And what of the songs themselves? What do they tell us? Simply—everything. Everything from the first conversation between a boy and a girl to an age-old dialogue between man and the Almighty. From a happy rabbi to an outraged socialist. From the hand holding the plow to the hand holding the gun. From parents to children and from children back to parents. From the blacksmith shop of the *shtetl* to the sweatshop of New York. From *shul* to ghetto to concentration camp . . . everything.

Hopefully the translations have preserved some of the *tam*—the taste—of the originals. Translating songs is akin to assembling a three-dimensional jigsaw puzzle: rhyme, meter, meaning, literary level (slang, localisms, dialect, etc.), and, of course, singability—all have to be taken into account and dealt with harmoniously. The songs in their original Yiddish vary widely in all these categories. Like folk songs the world over, the number of syllables in corresponding lines of successive verses may not be the same. The experienced interpreter will know instinctively just how to improvise to make melody and irregular lyrics fit together. The translator has to decide if he should consistently follow these irregularities, as it were, or try to make all the lyrics fit the music of the first verse.

Another set of problems arises when translating the works of poet-songwriters who concerned themselves with intricate rhyming patterns, internal rhymes, abrupt changes in meter and other schooled poetical devices. For example, the song *"Di Soche"* (page 72), with its twelve-line verse, presents the following rhyme scheme:

a a b c d d d c e e e c

The nine-line verses of *"Es Brent"* (page 184) are rhymed

a a b c c b d d b

The musical arrangements have been kept simple and the chords should be well within the grasp of amateur guitarists. Though the preponderance of the songs are in minor keys, they should not be thought of automatically as all sad and mournful. Let your interpretation of these gems of Jewish folk songs flow naturally from the meaning and spirit of the lyrics.

One final thought:

Lechayim yidelech!
Lachayim briderlech!
Zingt zhe, trinkt zhe,
Ale in a guter sho!
To, lomir hulyenen,
Arayn zich kulyenen
In dem ganeydn—
Bolshe nitshevo!*

*See page 100.

viii

About the Photographs

With two notable exceptions, the photographs in this book are a sort of family album. They show scenes from the lives of the maternal and paternal branches of my family and my wife's family, both in Europe and America, as well as the fruit of those branches: my children and their friends. They span five generations and about one hundred years—from beards to blue jeans, from Bessarabia to the Bronx, and from White Russia to Westchester.

Yet as personal as these pictures are, they somehow transcend the microcosm of the lives of these intertwined families—those faces from long ago and far away staring impassively into the lens, all dressed up in their *shabesdike* best. They are the *bubas* and *zeydas*, the *mames* and *tates*, who lovingly brought up their children in the tsarist Pale of settlement under conditions of great difficulty and uncertainty, and who finally moved whole families (again under conditions of great difficulty and uncertainty) to France . . . England . . . America.

The exceptions to this family album are indeed notable. In 1938 the eminent Jewish scholar and historian Dr. Irving Levitas visited Poland. On the very eve of the long night he brought out a series of photographs of Jewish life taken in and around Warsaw. They show unremarkable Jews doing unremarkable tasks. Just a bunch of ordinary snapshots of ordinary people—just an ordinary lost civilization, like the Etruscans or the Incas: Polish Jews.

More terrible yet are the photos taken by Rabbi J. X. Cohen in Vilna, under the Nazi occupation, probably in 1943. Here we see the Holocaust in operation: snow-covered streets; Jews, wearing their yellow stars, pushing, pulling, carrying all their belongings. Where are they coming from? All the outlying villages are being emptied of Jews, being made *judenrien*; all Jews ordered into the Vilna ghetto. We know what happens next.

About the Transliterations

Pronunciation in Yiddish varies somewhat with geographical location. A Polish Jew does not pronounce all vowels in the same manner as a Russian Jew. Standard spoken Yiddish does not exist. Any attempt at transliteration, therefore, comes up against the problem of regional speech patterns. I have tried to maintain a measure of consistency in basing the transliterations upon my perceptions of the sounds of the language. The result is very close to guidelines established in publications of the Workmen's Circle and YIVO.

		English	Yiddish
Vowels	a	f*a*r	b*a*n
	e	b*e*d	Yank*e*le (always voiced at end of word)
	i	*i*t	b*i*ter
	o	m*o*ther	h*o*b
	u	t*o*	d*u*
Diphthongs	ay	sk*y*	m*ay*n
	ey	th*ey*	z*ey*
	oy	b*oy*	*oy*f
Consonant combinations	ch	Ba*ch* (German)	i*ch*
	ts, tz	ge*ts*	*ts*u, shvar*tz*
	tsh	hi*tch*	*tsh*iribim
	zh	mea*s*ure	*zh*e
	r	Pa*r*is (French r)	*r*ebe

I have allowed myself the luxury of three inconsistencies because the currency of the words in question in current English orthography:

Balal*ai*ka instead of balal*ay*ka
Sholem Al*ei*chem instead of Sholem Al*ey*chem
Mark *W*arshawsky instead of Mark *V*arsha*v*sky

CONTENTS

Forshpays vii
About the Photographs ix
About the Transliterations xi

Love

Fun Vanen Heybt Zich On A Libe? (How Does a Love Start?) 3
Vuszhe Vils Tu? (What Do You Want?) 4
Di Gilderne Pave (The Golden Peacock) 6
A Libe, A Libe (A Love, Yes, a Love) 8
A Cholem (A Dream) 10
Margaritkes (Daisies) 11
Tum Balalaika 15
Papir Iz Doch Vays (Oh, Paper Is White) 17
Libster Mayner (My Sweetheart) 18
Yomi, Yomi 19
Her Nor, Du Shayn Maydele (Listen, My Sweet Pretty Girl) 20
Gey Ich Mir Shpatsirn (Once I Went Out Strolling) 22
Du Meydele, Du Fayns (You Pretty Little Girl) 24
Lomir Zich Iberbetn (Let's Make Up) 26
Di Zun Vet Arunter Geyn (The Sun Will Soon Set) 28
Unter a Kleyn Beymele (Sitting 'Neath a Little Tree) 30
Oy, Dortn, Dortn (Away Out Yonder) 32
Bin Ich Mir Gegangen Fishelech Koyfn (I Went to the Market, to Buy Some
  Fish There) 33
Biztu Mit Mir Broygez? (Are You Angry With Me?) 34
Oyfn Ganikl (Upon the Doorstep) 36
Shvartse Karshelech (Black Cherries) 38

Children

Jamele 43
Unter Dem Kinds Vigele (Under Baby's Little Crib) 44
Shlof, Mayn Feygele (Sleep, My Little Bird) 45

Oyfn Pripetshok (On the Hearth)   46

Shlof, Mayn Kind (Sleep, My Child)   48

Vigndig a Fremd Kind (Rocking Someone's Else's Child)   51

Rozhinkes Mit Mandlen (Raisins and Almonds)   53

Dray Yingelech (Three Little Boys)   54

Bay Dem Shtetl Shteyt a Shtibl (In the Village There's a Cabin)   56

O, Ir Kleyne Lichtelech (Oh, You Little Candle Lights)   59

Hulyet, Hulyet, Kinderlech (Play, My Dearest Little Ones)   60

Birobizhaner Viglid (Birobidjan Lullaby)   62

A Fidler (A Fiddler)   64

Lechayim!

In der Kuznye (In the Smithy)   66

Di Bord (The Beard)   68

Di Mechutonim Geyen (The Inlaws Are Arriving)   70

Di Soche (The Plow)   72

Shprayz Ich Mir (Walking Down the Highway)   74

Dos Lidl fun Broyt (The Song of Bread)   75

A Chazzandl oyf Shabes (A Cantor for the Sabbath)   76

Bayt Zhe Mir Oys a Finfuntsvantsiker (Change for Me This Twenty-
    Fiver)   78

Ale Mentshen Tantzendik (Folks Are at Their Dancingest)   79

A Glezele Lechayim (A Toast to Life)   70

Chatskele, Chatskele   82

Hey! Zhankoye   83

Hamentashn   84

Birobidjan   85

Vi Azoy Trinkt a Keyser Tey? (How Does a Tsar Drink Tea?)   86

Achtsik Er un Zibetsik Zi (Eighty He and Seventy She)   89

Di Mezinke Oysgegebn (My Youngest Daughter's Married)   90

Ch'bin a Bocher a Hultay (I'm a Wandering Fellow)   92

Kum Aher, Du Filozof (Come to Me, Philosopher)   93

Di Ban (The Train)   95

Sha! Shtil! (Shh! Quiet!)   96

Tshiribim   98

Lechayim! (To Life!)   100

Der Rebe Elimelech (Rabbi Elimelech)   103

It's Hard To Be A Jew

Moyshele, Mayn Fraynd (Moyshele, My Friend)   106
Tsum Hemerl (To the Hammer)   108
Lomir Ale Zingen a Zemerl (Everybody Sing a Little Song)   110
Hirsh Lekert   112
Dem Milners Trern (The Miller's Tears)   114
Keshenever Pogrom (Kishinev Pogrom)   117
Fonye Ganev (Fonye, the Thief)   118
Fonye Dinen Iz Zeyer Biter (Serving Fonye Is Very Bitter)   119
Fraytik in der Fri (Early Friday Morn)   120
Farvos Zol Zayn Mayn Chosn a Soldat? (Why Should They Make a Soldier of
   My Love?)   123
Zayzhe Mir Gezunt (I Must Say Farewell)   125
Yoshke Fort Avek (Yoshke's Leaving Now)   126
Dos Fertsnte Yor (In Nineteen-fourteen)   128
A Ganyeve (A Robbery)   130
Hot Rachmones (Have Compassion)   132
Mit a Nodl, On a Nodl (With a Needle, or Without One)   133
Zol Ich Zayn a Rov? (Should I Be a Rabbi?)   134
Maykomashmalon (What Does It Mean?)   136
Shlof Mayn Kind, Shlof Keseyder (Sleep My Child, Sleep Securely)   138
Ot Azoy Neyt a Shnayder (Stitch Away, Little Tailor)   139
Un Du Akerst (Oh, You Plow)   140
Dire Gelt (Rent Money)   141
Bulbes (Potatoes)   143
Bin Ich Mir a Shnayderl (I'm a Little Tailor)   144
Vi Zenen Mayne Yunge Yoren? (Where Are My Youthful Years?)   147

Amerike! Amerike!

Lidl fun Goldenem Land (Song of the Golden Land)   150
Shikt a Tiket (Send a Ticket)   152
Eyn Zach Vel Ich (One Thing I Ask)   154
Frahayt Statue (Statue of Liberty)   155
Kesl Gardn (Castle Garden)   156
Lebn Zol Kolombus (Long Life to Columbus)   158
Kolombus, Ich Hob Tsu Dir Gornit (Columbus, I Give You the
   First Prize)   160

Elis Ayland (Ellis Island)   161
New Yorker Trern (The Tears of New York)   162
Eyder Ich Leyg Mich Shlofn (No Sooner Do I Lie Down)   163
Mayn Rue Plats (My Resting Place)   164
Mayn Yingele (My Little Son)   166
Svetshop (Sweatshop)   168
Dem Pedlers Brivl (The Peddler's Letter)   170
Arbeter Froyen (You Working Women)   172
A Briv fun Amerike (A Letter from America)   175
In Kamf (In Struggle)   176
Vos Vet Zayn der Sof? (What Will Be the End?)   178
To Gey Zich Lernen Tantsn (Just Go and Learn to Dance Now)   180

The Holocaust

Es Brent (On Fire)   184
Unter di Churves fun Poyln (Under the Ruins of Poland)   186
Itsik Vitnberg   188
Aroys Iz in Vilne a Nayer Bafel (In Vilna Was Issued a
    Brand-New Decree)   190
Geto Lid (Ghetto Song)   192
Yeder Ruft Mich Zyamele (People Call Me Ziamele)   194
S'Dremlin Feygele (People Call Me Ziamele)   196
Yugnt-Himn (Youth Hymn)   198
Neyn, Neyn, Neyn (No, No, No)   201
Shtil di Nacht (Still the Night)   202
Zog Nit Keynmol (Never Say)   203
Ani Maamin (I Believe)   204

Basic guitar chords   206

Love

Wedding photograph from Sevastopol, Russia, 1894. The man was on leave from his army duties as a shoemaker to officers — hence his short haircut.

Chernia and Benish Mindlin shortly after their marriage in Orsha, Russia, in 1895.

FUN VANEN HEYBT ZICH ON A LIBE?
HOW DOES A LOVE START?

Gaily

Fun va - nen heybt zich on ___ a - li - be? Fun
How does a love start in the be - gin - ning? By

rey - dn, fun shmu - e - sn, fun la - chn. Un - dzer
talk - ing, by gos - sip - ing, by laugh - ter. Our

li - be hot zich on - ge - hoy - bn,
love did not start like the oth - ers,

1.
Gor fun an - de - re za - chn;
not what we both were af - ter;

2.
Un - dzer za - chn.
Our af - ter

C   G7
Dort geyen zich porelech tsvey,
C   E7   Am
Dort geyen zich porelech tsvey;
F   E
Libn, libn zey zich zeyer,
E7   Am
S'iz nishto keyn glaychn tsu zey.   2

C   G7
Genug shoyn mit mir tsu reydn,
C   E7   Am
Genug shoyn mit mir tsu shmuesn;
F   E
Fir mich shoyn op aheym,
E7   Am
Der tate vet di tir farshlisn.   2

C   G7
Aheym, Lyubtshe, vet ich dich opfirn,
C   E7   Am
Baym glekele vestu onklingen,
F   E
A lid vel ich oys undz beydn machn,
E7   Am
Di gantse velt zol fun undz zingen!   2

C   G7
Now, those loving couples you see,
C   E7   Am
Now, those loving couples you see,
F   E
Oh, they love each other deeply—
E7   Am
No equal to them can there be.   2

C   G7
Now, let's put an end to this talking,
C   E7   Am
I've heard all your stories before.
F   E
It's time to take me home,
E7   Am
My father will soon lock the door.   2

C   G7
Dear Lybutshe, I will take you home now,
C   E7   Am
The doorbell you soon will be ringing.
F   E
A song I will write of our feelings,
E7   Am
About us the world will be singing.   2

3

VUSZHE VILS TU?
WHAT DO YOU WANT?

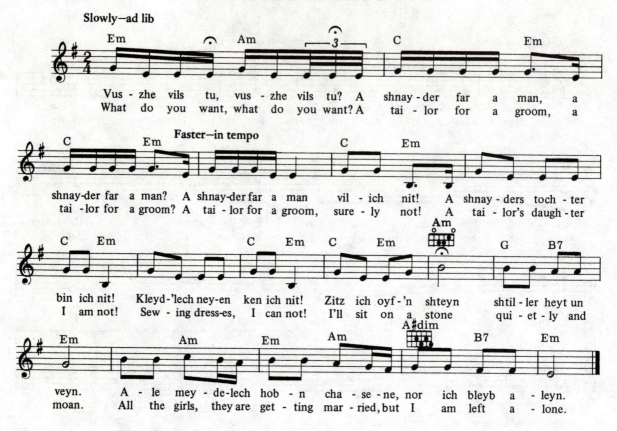

Slowly—ad lib

Vus-zhe vils tu, vus-zhe vils tu? A shnay-der far a man, a
What do you want, what do you want? A tai-lor for a groom, a

Faster—in tempo

shnay-der far a man? A shnay-der far a man vil-ich nit! A shnay-ders toch-ter
tai-lor for a groom? A tai-lor for a groom, sure-ly not! A tai-lor's daugh-ter

bin ich nit! Kleyd-'lech ney-en ken ich nit! Zitz ich oyf-'n shteyn shtil-ler heyt un
I am not! Sew-ing dress-es, I can not! I'll sit on a stone qui-et-ly and

veyn. A-le mey-de-lech hob-n cha-se-ne, nor ich bleyb a-leyn.
moan. All the girls, they are get-ting mar-ried, but I am left a-lone.

Em	Am		Em	Am
Vuszhe vils tu, vuszhe vils tu?			What do you want, what do you want?	

C	Em		C	Em
A shuster far a man?			A cobbler for a groom?	

C	Em		C	Em
A shuster far a man?			A cobbler for a groom?	

C	Em		C	Em
A shuster far a man vil ich nit!			A cobbler for a groom, surely not!	

C	Em		C	Em
A shusters tochter bin ich nit!			A cobbler's daughter, I am not!	

C	Em		C	Em
Shich lotn ken ich nit!			Patching shoes, I cannot!	

C	Em	Am	C	Em	Am
Zits ich oyf'n shteyn			I'll sit on a stone		

G	B7	Em	G	B7	Em
Shtiller hayt un veyn:			And I'll weep and moan:		

Am	Em	Am	Am	Em	Am
Ale meydelach hobn chasene,			All the girls, they are getting married,		

A#dim	B7	Em	A#dim	B7	Em
Nor ich blayb aleyn!			But I am left alone.		

4

```
Em        Am
Vuszhe vils tu, vuszhe vils tu?

   C          Em
A rebbn far a man?

   C          Em
A rebbn far a man?

                     C      Em
       A rebbn far a man vil ich doch!

                     C      Em
       A rebbns tochter bin ich doch!

                C      Em
       Toyre lernen ken ich doch!

   C      Em Am
Zits ich oyf'n dach

   G   B7  Em
Un kuk arup un lach:

      Am      Em   Am
   Ale meydelach hobn chasene,

A#dim  B7    Em
Ich mit zey baglach!
```

```
Em        Am
What do you want, what do you want?

   C          Em
A rabbi for a groom?

   C          Em
A rabbi for a groom?

                          C      Em
       A rabbi for a groom—that's for me!

                            C      Em
       I'm a rabbi's daughter, don't you see!

                     C      Em
       Torah learning—certainly!

   C      Em Am
I am flying high,

   G   B7  Em
Laugh until I cry:

      Am      Em   Am
   All the girls are getting married,

A#dim  B7    Em
And now so am I!
```

DI GILDERNE PAVE
THE GOLDEN PEACOCK

Slow—ballad style

Es kumt ge - floy - gen di gil - der - ne pa - ve, Fun a frem - den
A gold - en pea - cock once came a fly - ing, From a - far she

land,_____ Fun a frem - den_ land. Hot zi far - loy - ren dem
came,_____ From a - far she_ came. And she did lose her one

gil - der - nem fe - der, Mit a groys - sen_ shand; Hot
bright gol - den feath - er, To her bit - ter_ shame; And

zi far - loy - ren dem gil - der-nem fe - der, Mit a groys - sen_ shand.
she did lose her one bright gol-den feath - er, To her bit ter_ shame.

Em Am A7 D7
Es iz nit azoy der gilderne feder,

G D7 G D7
Vi di pave aleyn,

G D7 G D7
Vi di pave aleyn.

G B7 Em AmEmAmEm B7
Es iz nit azoy der ey - dem,

EmAmDm   E
Vi di tochter aleyn;

D7 G B7 EmAmEmAmEm B7
Es iz nit azoy der ey - dem,

EmAmDm   E
Vi di tochter aleyn.

Em Am A7 D7
It's not so much the golden feather,

G   D7   G D7
As the peacock herself,

G   D7   G D7
As the peacock herself.

G B7 Em Am EmAmEm B7
It's not so much the son-in-law,

EmAm Dm   E
As the daughter herself;

D7 G B7 Em Am EmAmEm B7
It's not so much the son-in-law,

EmAmDm   E
As the daughter herself.

Em Am   A7 D7
Vi es iz biter, mayn libe muter,

  G   D7   G D7
A feygele oyf dem yam,

  G   D7   G D7
A feygele oyf dem yam.

  G B7 EmAm   EmAmEmB7
Azoy iz biter, mayn libe muter,

     Em Am   Dm   E
Az me kumt un tsu a shlechtn man;

D7 G B7 EmAm   EmAmEmB7
Azoy iz biter, mayn libe muter,

     Em   Am   Dm   E
Az me kumt un tsu a shlechtn man.

   Em Am   A7 D7
Vi es iz biter, mayn libe muter,

   G   D7 G D7
A feygele on a nest,

   G   D7 G D7
A feygele on a nest.

   G B7 EmAm   EmAmEmB7
Azoy iz biter, mayn libe muter,

  Em Am Dm   E
Shver un shvigers kest;

D7 G B7 EmAm   EmAmEmB7
Azoy iz biter, mayn libe muter,

  Em Am Dm   E
Shver un shvigers kest.

   Em Am   A7 D7
Vi es is biter, mayn liber muter,

   G   D7 G D7
A shtibele on a tir,

   G   D7 G D7
A shtibele on a tir.

   G B7 EmAm   EmAmEmB7
Azoy iz biter, mayn libe muter,

EmAmDm   E
Lebn mir on dir;

D7 G B7 EmAm   EmAmEmB7
Azoy iz biter, mayn libe muter,

EmAmDm   E
Lebn mir on dir.

   Em Am   A7   D7
How it is bitter, my dearest mother,

   G   D7 G D7
A bird upon the sea,

   G   D7 G D7
A bird upon the sea.

   G B7 EmAm   EmAm Em B7
So it is bitter, my dearest mother,

     Em Am   Dm   E
When my man's cruel to me;

D7 G B7 EmAm   EmAm Em B7
So it is bitter, my dearest mother,

     Em Am   Dm   E
When my man's cruel to me.

   Em Am   A7   D7
How it is bitter, my dearest mother,

   G   D7 G D7
A bird without a nest,

   G   D7 G D7
A bird without a nest.

  G B7 EmAm   EmAmEm B7
So it is bitter, my dearest mother,

  Em Am Dm   E
To eat my in-law's crust;

D7 G B7 EmAm   EmAmEm B7
So it is bitter, my dearest mother,

  Em AmDm   E
To eat my in-law's crust.

   Em Am   A7   D7
How it is bitter, my dearest mother,

   G   D7 G D7
A house without a door,

   G   D7 G D7
A house without a door.

   G B7 EmAm   EmAm Em B7
So it is bitter, my dearest mother,

  Em Am Dm E
To see you nevermore.

D7 G B7 EmAm   EmAm Em B7
So it is bitter, my dearest mother,

   Em Am Dm   E
To see you nevermore.

A LIBE, A LIBE
A LOVE, YES, A LOVE

A li - be, a li - be iz gut tzu fi - ren, Mit a
A love, yes, a love is ve - ry good to have, With a

mentsh — o - ber nisht mit dir. Ge - vald, ich vel durch dir kra -
real man, not you, don't you see? My God, you'll send me to an

pi - ren! Vos hos tu dich ayn - ge - libt in mir? Ge -
ear - ly grave! Why did you fall so in love with me? My

vald, ich vel durch dir kra - pi - ren! Vos hos tu dich any - ge - libt in mir?
God, you'll send me to an ear - ly grave! Why did you fall so in love with me?

Dm Gm A
Vos shteystu unter mayne fenster,

Gm A7 Dm A7
Azoy vi a zelner far der tir?

D7 Gm
Tsu bin ich den di tayreste, di shenste?

Dm A7 Dm A7
Vos hostu zich ayngelibt in mir?

D7 Gm
Tsu bin ich den di tayreste, di shenste?

Dm A7 Dm
Vos hostu zich ayngelibt in mir?

Dm Gm A
You stand by my window and you never rest.

Gm A7 Dm A7
At my door, you're all I ever see.

D7 Gm
Am I your dearest and your prettiest?

Dm A7 Dm A7
Why did you fall so in love with me?

D7 Gm
Am I your dearest and your prettiest?

Dm A7 Dm
Why did you fall so in love with me?

```
  Dm        Gm              A
A fayer hot gedarft dos hoyz farbrenen,

 Gm      A7          Dm A7
Eyder ich hob dich dort gezeyn.

   D7                  Gm
Der tayvl hot mich gedarft tsunemen,

 Dm            A7       Dm A7
Eyder du host zich ayngelibt in mir!

   D7                  Gm
Der tayvl hot mich gedarft tsunemen,

 Dm            A7       Dm
Eyder du host zich ayngelibt in mir!
```

```
   Dm     Gm        A
Vest krugn a shenere un a besere,

    Gm     A7        Dm A7
Zi vet zayn kluger noch far mir.

 D7                  Gm
A berye vet zi oych zayn, a gresere;

 Dm           A7      Dm A7
Vuszhe hostu zich ayngelibt in mir?

  D7                 Gm
A berye vet zi oych zayn, a gresere;

 Dm           A7      Dm
Vuszhe hostu zich ayngelibt in mir?
```

```
  Dm Gm                   A
A fire should have burned that house down,

 Gm     A7          Dm A7
Before I ever you did see.

  D7                   Gm
The devil should have taken me away,

 Dm           A7       Dm A7
Before you fell so in love with me.

  D7                   Gm
The devil should have taken me away,

 Dm          A7        Dm
Before you fell so in love with me.
```

```
  Dm      Gm              A
A prettier and better girl you'll surely find.

   Gm      A7          Dm A7
She'll be wiser than I could ever be.

  D7                    Gm
More skillfull and with a much finer mind;

  Dm          A7        Dm A7
Why did you fall so in love with me?

  D7                    Gm
More skillfull and with a much finer mind;

  Dm         A7         Dm
Why did you fall so in love with me?
```

A CHOLEM
A DREAM

By S. GINZBURG
and P. MAREK

Brightly

A cho-lem a cho-lem hot zich mir ge-cho-lemt, A
I dreamed it, I dreamed it, just last night I dreamed it, I

cho-lem, lyu-be, hot zich mir ge-dacht, oy, ge-dacht! Mit
dreamed it. Lyu-be, clear-ly I did see, I did see! With

day-ne shvar-tse oy-gn hos-tu mich tsu-ge-tsoy-gn, Un
your dark eyes of fi-re you wa-kened my de-si-re, You

far a men-tshn hos-tu mich ge-macht. Mit macht.
went and made a new man out of me. With me.

Em   Am
Ich es nisht, ich trink nisht, ich shlof nisht durch di

Em
necht,

Am   D7   G D7   G
Un benken, Lyube, benk ich noch dir, oy, noch dir!

G   Em   Am
Ven ich dermon zich, dushe, on dir, mayn

Em
   tayer-lebn,   2

C   Am B7   Em
Geyen mir di koyches oys noch dir!

Em   Am
I don't eat, I don't drink, I don't sleep all the

Em
night,

Am   D7   G   D7   G
I'm longing, Lyube, longing just for you—just for you.

G   Em   Am
And when I think, o honey, of you, my dearest

Em
   sweetheart,   2

C   Am B7   Em
I lose all my strength, what can I do?

Em   Am   Em
Shpatsirn, oy, Lyube, zaynen mir gegangen,

Am   D7   G D7   G
In droysn iz gevezn a shney, oy, a shney!

G   Em   Am
Gedenkstu, Lyube sheyne, du host mir tray

Em
   geshvorn,   2

C   Am B7   Em
Tsum sof hostu gor andere tsvey!

Em   Am   Em
A-strolling, o Lyube, we two went a-strolling.

Am   D7   G D7   G
Outside was the softly falling snow—yes, the snow,

G   Em   Am
Remember, dearest Lyube, you swore that you'd

Em
   be faithful,   2

C   Am B7   Em
But now with two others you do go.

10

MARGARITKES
DAISIES

Words b

In vel - dl baym tay - chl dort zay - nen ge -
Down in the green for - est a - long the calm

vak - sn mar - ga - rit - ke - lach el - ent un kleyn. _____ Vi
riv - er, lit - tle dai - sies grow grace - ful and small. _____ Like

kleyn - in - ke zu - nen mit vay - sin - ke shtra - ln, mit
ti - ny bright suns bear - ing lit - tle white sun - beams, with

vays_ in - ke tra _ la la la. _____ Vi la. _____
lit - tle white tra _ la la la. _____ Like la. _____

Am   E7   Am
Gegangen iz Chavele, shtil un farcholemt
  C   G7   C E7
Tzulozn di gold-blonde tsep.
  Am   Dm   Am Dm
Dos heldzl antbloyzt un gemurmlt-gezungen
  Am   E7   Am
A lidele: tra la la la.   ]2

  Am   E7
Es kumt ir antkegn a bocher a
    Am
   shvartser,
  C   G7   C E7
Mit lokn mit shvartse, vi pech;
  Am   Dm Am   Dm
Er flamt mit di oygn un entfert ir lustig,
  Am   E7   Am
Un entfert ir: tra la la la.   ]2

      Am   E7   Am
Young Chave was walking along and daydreaming,
    C   G7   C E7
Her blond braids were hanging down free.
    Am   Dm   Am Dm
Her collar unbuttoned, and quietly humming
    Am   E7   Am
A melody—tra la la la.   ]2

      Am   E7
Then came out to meet her a boy, young and
      Am
     handsome,
    C   G7   C E7
With black curly hair, dark as pitch.
    Am   Dm   Am   Dm
His eyes, how they sparkle—he speaks to her gaily,
    Am   E7   Am
He speaks to her—tra la la la.   ]2

(continued)

11

```
      Am                     E7
"Vos zuchstu do meydl? Vos hos tu

        Am
        ferloyrn?
      C      G7      C    E7
Vos vilstu gefinen in groz?"

        Am     Dm      Am     Dm
"Ich zuch margaritkes," far'roytlt zich Chave,  ⎤
                                                ⎥ 2
      Am      E7    Am                          ⎦
Far' roytlt zich tra la la la.
```

```
      Am                         E7
"Say, what are you seeking? Can you have lost

        Am
        something?
      C      G7        C      E7
And why do you look in the grass?"

        Am     Dm      Am       Dm
"I'm looking for daisies,"said Chave, all blushing.  ⎤
                                                     ⎥ 2
      Am      E7    Am                               ⎦
All blushing and tra la la la.
```

```
        Am                        E7   Am
"Du zuchst noch? un ich hob shoyn take gefunen

      C        G7      C   E7
Di shenste margaritke in vald,

        Am     Dm      Am    Dm
A margaritke mit tsep un mit oygn safirn,   ⎤
                                            ⎥ 2
      Am      E7    Am                      ⎦
Mit eygelech tra la la la."
```

```
        Am                        E7   Am
"And are you still looking? But I have discovered

      C        G7      C  E7
The prettiest daisy of all.

        Am     Dm      Am       Dm
A daisy with braids and with eyes of bright sapphire,  ⎤
                                                       ⎥ 2
      Am      E7    Am                                 ⎦
With sapphire eyes—tra la la la."
```

```
        Am                       E7
"Neyn, ch'ob shoyn margaritkes, ich hob zich

        Am
        fargesn—
      C        G7        C      E7
Ich zuch . . . do nisht vayt iz a kval . . ."

      Am     Dm      Am
"Der kval iz geshlosh, on mir blaybstu   ⎤
                                         ⎥
        Dm                               ⎥ 2
        durshtig,                        ⎥
      Am      E7    Am                   ⎦
Baym kvelchele tra la la la."
```

```
        Am                    E7
"No, I've got some daisies, I'd almost

        Am
        forgotten.
      C        G7      C        E7
I'm looking—nearby is a spring . . ."

      Am     Dm      Am
"The spring is all dried up—without me there's  ⎤
                                                ⎥
        Dm                                      ⎥ 2
        nothing,                                ⎥
      Am      E7    Am                          ⎦
Without me there's tra la la la."
```

```
        Am                      E7      Am
"Ich vil gornisht trinken, ich zuch mir a shotn,

      C       G7        C   E7
Di zun bakt arayn azoy heys . . ."

        Am     Dm      Am     Dm
"Mayne hor zenen shvartser un kiler vi shotns  ⎤
                                               ⎥ 2
      Am   E7    Am                            ⎦
In veldele tra la la la."
```

```
        Am                      E7      Am
"I'm not really thirsty, it's shade that I'm seeking,

      C       G7        C   E7
The sun is so terribly hot."

        Am     Dm      Am       Dm
"My hair is much darker and cooler than shadows,  ⎤
                                                  ⎥ 2
      Am      E7    Am                            ⎦
Than forest shade—tra la la la."
```

Am   E7
"O, loz mich, men tor nisht; di mame zogt,

     Am
   m'tor nisht,

C   G7   C   E7
Mayn mame iz alt un iz beyz."

   Am   Dm   Am   Dm
"Vu mame? Vos mame? Do zenen nor boymer,

   Am   E7   Am
Nor boymelech tra la la la."   ] 2

Am   E7
"Oh, leave me—we must not. My mother

     Am
   forbids it.

C   G7   C   E7
My mother is old and is mean."

   Am   Dm   Am   Dm
"Where mother? What mother? I only see trees here,

   Am   E7   Am
Just little trees—tra la la la."   ] 2

   Am   E7
"Men zet"–"Keyner zet nisht!" "Men hert!"

     Am
   "Keyner hert nisht,

C   G7   C   E7
Dos veldl iz blind un gedicht . . .

   Am   Dm   Am   Dm
Umarim mich, zise, du zest: ich bin ruhig,

   Am   E7   Am
Ich kush dich nor—tra la la la."   ] 2

   Am   E7
"They'll see us!" "Who's looking?" "They'll hear

     Am
   us!" "Who's listening?

C   G7   C   E7
The forest is blind and is dense.

   Am   Dm   Am   Dm
Embrace me, my sweet one. You see, I am gentle.

   Am   E7   Am
I'll just kiss you—tra la la la."   ] 2

   Am   E7
"Du libst mich?" "Ich lib dich." "Du shemst

     Am
   zich?" "Ich shem mich!"

C   G7   C   E7
"O, lib mich un shem dich un shvayg,

Am   Dm   Am
Un ze vi es mishn zich pech-shvartse

     Dm
   kroynen

Am   E7   Am
Mit goldene . . . tra la la la."   ] 2

   Am   E7
"You love me?" "I love you!" "You're bashful?"

     Am
   "I'm bashful!"

C   G7   C   E7
"Oh, love me, be bashful and still,

Am   Dm   Am   Dm
And see how they mingle, the black and the golden

   crowns,

Am   E7   Am
Golden crowns—tra la la la."   ] 2

   Am   E7   Am
Di zun iz fargangen, der bocher farshvunden,

   C   G7   C   E7
Un Chavele zitst noch in vald,

   Am   Dm   Am   Dm
Zi kukt fun dervaytns un mermit farcholemt

   Am   E7   Am
Dos lidele: tra la la la.   ] 2

   Am   E7   Am
The sun has gone under, and gone is the young man,

   C   G7   C   E7
And Chave still sits in the woods,

   Am   Dm   Am   Dm
She looks in the distance and dreamily murmurs

   Am   E7   Am
The melody—tra la la la.   ] 2

Three sisters in Kilia, Bessarabia, Russia, 1903

TUM BALALAIKA

Shteyt a boch - er un __ er tracht, Tracht und tracht di gan - tze nacht;
A young man is deep __ in thought, And he won - ders whom __ he ought

Ve - men tsu ne - men, un nit far - she - men, Ve - men, tsu ne - men, un nit far she - men.
To take as wife for all of his life, To take __ as wife for all of his life. __

Chorus

Tum ba - la, tum ba - la, tum ba - la - lai - ka, Tum ba - la,

tum ba - la, tum ba - la - lai - ka, Tum ba - la - lai - ka,

Shpil ba - la - lai - ka, Tum ba - la - lai ka, Frey - lich zol zayn.
Play ba - la - lai - ka, Play ba - la - lai ka, let there be joy.

Am E Meydl, meydl, ich vil bay dir fregn,	Am E Tell me, maiden, I'd like to know,
E7 Am Vos ken vaksn, vaksn on regn?	E7 Am What it is needs no rain to grow?
Dm Am Vos ken brenen un nit oyfheren?	Dm Am What's not consumed although it's burning?
Dm E E7 Am Vos ken beynkn, veynen on treren? *Chorus*	Dm E E7 Am What weeps no tears although it's yearning? *Chorus*
Am E Narisher bocher, vos darfst du fregn,	Am E You foolish boy, didn't you know,
E7 Am A shteyn ken vaksn, vaksn on regn.	E7 Am A stone does not need rain to grow?
Dm Am A libe ken brenen un nit oyfheren,	Dm Am A love's not consumed although it's burning,
Dm E E7 Am A hartz ken beynken, veynen on treren. *Chorus*	Dm E E7 Am A heart weeps no tears although it's yearning. *Chorus*

15

Class picture from Dubrovno, Russia, 1912

PAPIR IZ DOCH VAYS
OH, PAPER IS WHITE

Pa - pir iz doch vays, un tint iz doch shvarts. Tsu
Oh, pa-per is white, and ink, black as night. To

dir, mayn zis le - ben, tsit doch mayn harts. Ch'volt
you, my dear sweet - heart, my heart takes its flight. I'd

shten - dig ge ze - sen dray teg noch a - nand, Tsu
will - ing - ly wait - for three days I would stand, To

ku - shn dayn sheyn po - nim, un tsu hal - tn dayn hant.
kiss your fair face and to hold your dear hand.

Am Dm   E7   Am
Nechtn banacht bin ich oyf a chasene geven.
      F   G7   C
Fil sheyne meydelach hob ich dort gezen.
G7   E7   Am F   G7 C
Fil sheyne meydelach—tsu dir kumt nisht gor—
    F   Dm   E7   Am
Tsu dayne shvartse eygelach, tsu dayne shvartse hor.

   Am Dm   E7   Am
Ach du liber Got, varf mir nisht arop,
         F   G7   C
Glaych mich nit tsu keyn beymele un nit tsu keyn slop.
   G7   E7Am F G7 C
Dos beymele az es blit iz doch zeyer sheyn;
   F   Dm   E7   Am
Vi helft mir shoyn Got mir dir tsu der chupe tsu geyn.

      Am   Dm   E7   Am
Last night to a wedding I went without care.
         F   G7   C
A room full of pretty girls I did see there.
G7   E7   Am F G7 C
A room full of pretty girls—but none to compare
    F   Dm   E7   Am
With your pretty coal-black eyes, and your raven hair.

     Am   Dm E7   Am
Oh please, dearest God, do not cast me down.
         F   G7   C
I'm not like a tree or a stick in the ground.
   G7   E7 Am F G7 C
A tree when it blooms is lovely to see;
   F   Dm   E7   Am
With God's help, my darling, my bride you will be.

17

LIBSTER MAYNER
MY SWEETHEART

Words by **ABARBAREL**
Music by **BEN YOMEN**

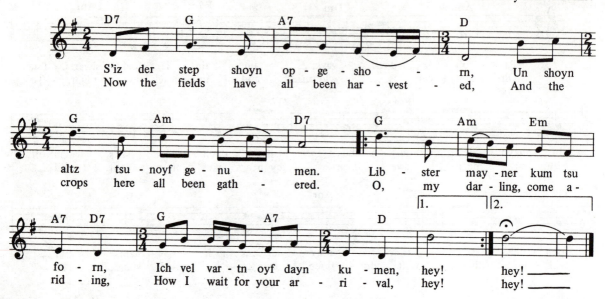

S'iz der step shoyn op-ge-sho - rn, Un shoyn
Now the fields have all been har-vest-ed, And the

altz tsu-noyf ge-nu - men. Lib - ster may-ner kum tsu
crops here all been gath - ered. O, my dar-ling, come a-

fo - rn, Ich vel var-tn oyf dayn ku-men, hey! hey! _____
rid-ing, How I wait for your ar - ri-val, hey! hey! _____

D7 G A7   D
Un di karshn, libster mayner,

    G Am D7
Zaynen shvartze vi dayne oygn.

G Am Em A7 D7
Ongeshotn oyf di beymer,

G   A7   D
Un di tsvaygn zich aych boygn, hey!   ]2

D7 G A7   D
Kum tsuforn, libster mayner,

    G Am D7
Un genug shoyn undz tsu troymen.

G Am Em A7D7
Rayf un tsaytig iz mayn libe

G   A7   D
Vi s'iz tsaytig mayne floymen, hey!   ]2

D7 G A7   D
And the cherries, o, my sweetheart,

    G Am D7
Like your eyes, they glisten darkly.

G Am Em A7 D7
Trees are covered over with them,

G   A7   D
And their branches, they bend to you, hey!   ]2

D7 G A7   D
Come a-riding, o, my sweetheart,

    G Am D7
Put an end to all my dreaming.

G Am Em A7D7
For my love is ripe and ready,

G   A7   D
Like the plums that are so juicy, hey!   ]2

YOMI, YOMI

Yo - mi, Yo - mi, zing mir a li - de - le, Vos dos mey de - le
Yo - mi, Yo - mi, sing me a lit - tle song, Tell me what do you

vil? Dos mey - de - le vil a por shi - che - lech hob - n,
want? Does my lit - tle girl want a new pair of shoes?

Chorus

Darf men geyn dem shus - ter - l zog - n. Neyn, ma - men - yu,
Let's go tell the cob - bler the news._____ No, ma - ma, dear,

neyn, Du kenst mich nit far - shteyn. Du veyst nit vos ich meyn.
no, That's not the way to go, I nev - er told you so.

Em   Am
Yomi, Yomi, zing mir a lidele,

Em   B7   Em
Vos dos meydele vil?

                C
Dos meydele vil a kleydele hobn,

Em   Am
Darf men geyn dem shnayderl zogn. *Chorus*

Em   Am
Yomi, Yomi, zing mir a lidele,

Em   B7   Em
Vos dos meydele vil?

            C
Dos meydele vil a chosendl hobn,

Em   Am
Darf men geyn dem shadchendl zogn.

Final chorus:

Em B7   Em
Yo, mamenyu, yo,

        B7   Em
Du veyst shoyn vos ich meyn,

    Am   B7   Em
Du kenst mich shoyn farshteyn!

Em   Am
Yomi, Yomi, sing me a little song,

Em   B7   Em
Tell me what do you want?

                C
Does my little girl want a brand-new dress?

Em   Am
Well, I know the tailor's address. *Chorus*

Em   Am
Yomi, Yomi, sing me a little song,

Em   B7   Em
Tell me, what do you want?

            C
Is it for a husband you're sighing,

Em   Am
To the matchmaker, quick, stop your crying.

Final chorus:

Em B7   Em
Yes, mama dear, yes,

        B7   Em
At last you understand

    Am   B7   Em
I really want a man.

19

HER NOR, DU SHAYN MAYDELE
LISTEN, MY SWEET PRETTY GIRL

Em
Her nor, du shayn maydele,
Em   Am
Her nor, du fayn maydele,
Em Am6 Em   Am Em
Vos vestu esn in aza vaytn veg?
G F EmAm B7 Em
Vos vestu esn in aza vaytn veg?

    D7   G B7 Em
Broyt mit zalts vel ich esn,
Cm G   Em6 C
Tate-mame vel ich fergesn;
   Em Am C
Abi mit dir tsuzamen zayn,
   Em Am B7 Em
Abi mit dir tsuzamen zayn.

Em   Am
Listen, my sweet pretty girl,
Em   Am
Listen, my dear pretty girl,
Em Am6 Em   Am   Em
What will you eat in such a faraway place?
   G F   EmAm   B7   Em
What will you eat in such a faraway place?

    D7   G   B7   Em
Bread and salt I'll eat with pleasure,
Cm   G   Em6   C
Parents, I'll forget forever;
   Em Am   C
As long as I can be with you,
   Em Am B7   Em
As long as I can be with you.

Em   Am
Her nor, du shayn maydele,

Em   Am
Her nor, du fayn maydele,

Em Am6 Em   Am Em
Oyf vos vestu shlofn in aza vaytn veg?

G   F   Em Am B7 Em
Oyf vos vestu shlofn in aza vaytn veg?

      D7   G   B7   Em
Ich bin noch a yunge froy,

     Cm   G   Em6   C
Ich ken shlofn oyf a bintl shtroy;

   Em Am   C
Abi mit dir tsuzamen zayn,

   Em Am   B7   Em
Abi mit dir tsuzamen zayn.

Em   Am
Listen, my sweet pretty girl,

Em   Am
Listen, my dear pretty girl,

Em Am6 Em   Am   Em
On what will you sleep in such a faraway place?

G   F   Em Am   B7   Em
On what will you sleep in such a faraway place?

      D7   G   B7   Em
I'm a young and healthy woman,

     Cm   G   Em6   C
I would sleep on straw with you, man,

   Em Am   C
As long as I can be with you,

   Em Am B7   Em
As long as I can be with you.

A Shayne Meydele in Riga, 1930

GEY ICH MIR SHPATSIRN
ONCE I WENT OUT STROLLING

Gey ich mir shpa - tsi - rn, } Tra - la - la - la - la - la. { Gey ich mir shpa -
Once I went out stroll - ing, } { Once I went out

tsi - rn, } Tra - la - la - la - la - la - la. { Ba - ge - gnt mich a bo - cher, a -
stroll - ing, } { I came a - cross a fel - low, a -

ha! A - ha! Ba - ge - gnt mich a bo - cher, a - ha!_____
ha! A - ha! I came a - cross a fel - low a - ha!_____

Em B7 Er zogt er vet mich nemen,	Em B7 He told me he would wed me,
Em B7 Tra la la la la la.	Em B7 Tra la la la la la.
G D7 Er zogt er vet mich nemen,	G D7 He told me he would wed me,
G D7 G Tra la la la la la la.	G D7 G Tra la la la la la la.
Em Am Er leygt es op oyf vinter,	Em Am But not before the winter,
B7 Aha! Aha!	B7 Aha! Aha!
Em Am B7 Er leygt es op oyf vinter,	Em Am B7 But not before the winter,
Em Aha!	Em Aha!

```
    Em        B7                    Em        B7
Der vinter is gekumen,          Well, winter is upon us,

       Em        B7                     Em        B7
    Tra la la la la la.             Tra la la la la la.

    G         D7                     G         D7
Der vinter iz gekumen,          Well, winter is upon us,

       G    D7    G                    G    D7    G
    Tra la la la la la la.          Tra la la la la la la.

    Em            Am                  Em            Am
Er hot mich nit genumen,        But he did break his promise,

       B7                             B7
    Aha! Aha!                       Aha! Aha!

    Em          Am B7                 Em          Am B7
Er hot mich nit genumen,        But he did break his promise,

       Em                             Em
    Aha!                            Aha!




    Em                 B7             Em                 B7
Itst vil er mich shoyn nemen,   And now he wants to take me,

       Em        B7                     Em        B7
    Tra la la la la la.             Tra la la la la la.

    G                 D7             G                 D7
Itst vil er mich shoyn nemen,   And now he wants to take me,

       G    D7    G                    G    D7    G
    Tra la la la la la la.          Tra la la la la la la.

    Em          Am                   Em          Am
Ober ich vil im nit kenen,      He really does mistake me,

       B7                             B7
    Aha! Aha!                       Aha! Aha!

    Em          Am B7                 Em          Am B7
Ober ich vil im nit kenen,      He really does mistake me,

       Em                             Em
    Aha!                            Aha!
```

DU MEYDEL, DU FAYNS
YOU PRETTY LITTLE GIRL

Du mey-de-le, du fayns, Du mey-de-le, du sheyns, Ich vel dir e-pes
You pret-ty lit-tle girl, You ap-ple of my eye, I have a rid-dle

fre-gn, A re-te-nish a kleyns: Vos iz he-cher fun____ a
for____ you, So an-swer it, please try: What is tall-er than____ a

hoyz? Un voz iz____ flink-er fun____ a moyz? Du na-ri-sher bo-cher, du
house? And what is____ fast-er than____ a mouse? You fool-ish____ boy, well, you

na-ri-sher chlop! Host doch nit kayn sey-chl - in__ dayn_ kop! Der roych iz
sure_ are so dense! Don't_ you_ have_ a__ bit of com-mon sense? For smoke is

hech-er fun ___ a hoyz. A katz iz___ flin-ker fun___ a moyz.
tall-er than___ a house. A cat is___ fast-er than___ a mouse.

Dm	E	Dm	E

Du meydele du fayns, du meydele du sheyns,

You pretty little girl, you apple of my eye,

Dm · · · · · E
Ich vel dir epes fregn, a retenish a kleyns:

Dm · · · · · E
I have a riddle for you, so answer it, please try:

Am · · · · · E
Vos ken fliyn on a fligl?

Am · · · · · E
What is wingless, but flies quick?

Dm · Am · Dm · E
Un vos ken moyern on a tsigl?

Dm · Am · Dm · E
And what can build without a brick?

Dm · E · Dm · E
Du narisher bocher, du narisher chlop!

Dm · E · Dm · E
You foolish boy, you sure are so dense!

Dm · · · · · E
Host doch nit keyn seychl in dayn kop!

Dm · · · · · E
Don't you have a bit of common sense?

Am · · · · · E
Der shney ken fliyn on a fligl,

Am · · · · · E
Snow is wingless, but flies quick.

Dm · Am · Dm · E
Un der frost ken moyern on a tsigl.

Dm · Am · Dm · E
Frost can build without a brick.

```
     Dm        E      Dm         E                      Dm        E     Dm          E
Du meydele du fayns, du meydele du sheyns,         You pretty little girl, you apple of my eye,
                       Dm          E                                Dm              E
Ich vel dir epes fregn, a retenish a kleyns:       I have a riddle for you, so answer it, please try:
Am                    E                            Am                    E
Vos fara keyser iz on a land?                      Where is the king who has no land?

   Dm     Am  Dm      E                               Dm         Am  Dm       E
Un vos fara vaser iz on zamd?                      And where is the water without sand?

          Dm        E      Dm       E                         Dm      E    Dm          E
   Du narisher bocher, du narisher chlop!             You foolish boy, you sure are so dense!
                      Dm          E                                   Dm              E
   Host doch nit keyn seychl in dayn kop!             Don't you have a bit of common sense?
       Am                    E                            Am                   E
   Der keyser fun harts hot nit keyn land.             The king of hearts, he has no land.

   Dm      Am  Dm        E                                Dm      Am    Dm      E
   Trern fun di oygn zenen on zamd.                    The tears that fall, they have no sand.
```

LOMIR ZICH IBERBETN
LET'S MAKE UP

Lo - mir zich i - ber - be - tn, i - ber - be - tn, Yos shtey - stu bay der
Let's make up once a - gain, let's make up now,__ Why stand there by the

tir? Vos shtey - stu bay der tir? Lo - mir zich i - ber - be - tn,
door? Why stand there at the door? Let's make up once a - gain, And

Kum a - rayn tsu mir. Lo - mir zich i - ber - be - tn, Kum a - rayn tsu mir.
we will fight no more. Let's make up once a - gain, And we will fight no more.

<table>
<tr><td>

E
Lomir zich iberbetn, iberbetn,

   E7   Am
Vos shteystu bay mayn fenster?

   E7   Am
Vos shteystu bay mayn fenster?

Dm   E
Lomir zich iberbetn,

Dm   E   ] 2
Bist bay mir der shenster.

</td><td>

E
Let's make up once again, let's make up now.

   E7   Am
Please don't stay outside,

   E7   Am
Please don't stay outside.

Dm   E
Let's make up once again,

    Dm   E   ] 2
For you're my lovely bride.

</td></tr>
<tr><td>

E
Lomir zich iberbetn, iberbetn,

   E7   Am
Koyf a por marantsn,

   E7   Am
Koyf a por marantsn.

Dm   E
Lomir zich iberbetn,

Dm   E   ] 2
Lomir geyen tantsn.

</td><td>

E
Let's make up once again, let's make up now.

   E7   Am
Oranges we'll buy,

   E7   Am
Oranges we'll buy.

Dm   E
Let's make up once again,

    Dm   E   ] 2
Go dancing, you and I.

</td></tr>
</table>

```
    E
Lomir zich iberbetn, iberbetn,

    E7          Am
Shtel dem samovar,

    E7          Am
Shtel dem samovar.

    Dm       E
Lomir zich iberbetn,

    Dm              E
Zay-zhe nisht kayn nar.          ] 2
```

```
    E
Let's make up once again, let's make up now.

    E7          Am
Heat the samovar,*

    E7          Am
Heat the samovar.

    Dm       E
Let's make up once again,

        Dm       E
How silly you now are.          ] 2
```

```
    E
Lomir zich iberbetn, iberbetn,

    E7                Am
Lomir nisht zayn vi geyrim,

    E7                Am
Lomir nisht zayn vi geyrim.

    Dm       E
Lomir zich iberbetn,

    Dm              E
Lomir zayn chaverim.          ] 2
```

```
    E
Let's make up once again, let's make up now.

    E7                Am
We're not like the others,

    E7                Am
We're not like the others.

    Dm       E
Let's make up once again,

        Dm       E
And let us just be lovers.          ] 2
```

*Samovar—typical Russian urn used for boiling water for tea.

DI ZUN VET ARUNTER GEYN
THE SUN WILL SOON SET

Words by **M. I. HELPERN**
Music by **BEN YOMEN**

Di zun vet a - run - ter geyn un - ter - n barg, Vet ku - men a
Be - hind the tall moun - tain the sun will soon set In si - lence the

shti - le di li - be tsu geyn, Vet ku - men a shti - le di
love that I feel will en - fold, In si - lence the love that I

li - be tsu geyn, Tsum u - met vos zitst oyf a gol - de - nem
feel _ will en - fold, The lone - li - ness seat - ed up - on stone of

shteyn, Un veynt far zich ey - nem a - leyn. _____ Tsum
gold, That weeps for it - self as of old. _____ The

u - met vos zitst oyf a gol - de - nem shteyn, Un
lone - li - ness seat - ed up - on stone of gold, That

veynt far zich ey - nem a - leyn. _____
weeps for it - self as of old. _____

```
    Dm                A7      Dm          Dm                    A7        Dm
Di zun vet arunter geyn untern barg,    Behind the tall mountain the sun will soon set,

   Gm            C7      F                  Gm                    C7         F
Vet kumen di goldene pave tsu flien,     The bright golden peacock will flutter our way,

   Gm            C7      F                  Gm                    C7         F
Vet kumen di goldene pave tsu flien,     The bright golden peacock will flutter our way,

    Dm           Gm Dm                     Dm                Gm     Dm
Un mitnemen vet zi uns ale ahin,         And take us all with him so far, far away,

        A7         Dm                            A7        Dm
Ahin vu di benkshaft vet tsien,          Wherever deep longing may say,

          Gm    Dm                                   Gm        Dm
Un mitnemen vet zi us ale ahin,          And take us all with him so far, far away,

   Bb      A7         Dm                    Bb        A7        Dm
Ahin vu di benkshaft vet tsien,          Wherever deep longing may say.


    Dm                A7      Dm          Dm                    A7        Dm
Di zun vet arunter geyn untern barg,    Behind the tall mountain the sun will soon set,

   Gm                  C7      F            Gm                C7       F
Vet kumen di nacht un vet zingen lyu, lyu, The night will arrive singing its lullaby,

   Gm                  C7      F            Gm                C7       F
Vet kumen di nacht un vet zingen lyu, lyu, The night will arrive singing its lullaby,

   Dm           Gm         Dm              Dm                  Gm      Dm
Ariber di oygen vos falen shoyn tsu,     And heavy with sleep, it will close every eye,

        A7      Dm                               A7       Dm
Tsu shlofn in eybiker ru,                Eternal rest is its sad cry.

          Gm         Dm                              Gm        Dm
Ariber di oygen vos falen shoyn tsu,     And heavy with sleep, it will close every eye,

   Bb     A7       Dm                       Bb       A7        Dm
Ariber in eybiker ru.                    Eternal rest is its sad cry.
```

UNTER A KLEYN BEYMELE
SITTING 'NEATH A LITTLE TREE

Dm
Er flegt, zogt er, gantse teg

Umgeyn, nit gegesn,
Gm
Dortn vu zi hot gevoynt,
A7　Dm
Shoyn opgezesn.
Gm
Dortn vu zi hot gevoynt,
A7　Dm
Shoyn opgezesn. *Chorus*

Dm
Shturem, vintn, regn, shney,

Keyn zach opgeshrokn.
Gm
Un di mame in der heym,
A7　Dm
Gevart hot mit a flokn.
Gm
Un di mame in der heym,
A7　Dm
Gevart hot mit a flokn. *Chorus*

Dm
He used to spend the whole day long

Wandering, not eating.
Gm
There, to where she used to live,
A7　　Dm
How his heart was beating.
Gm
There, to where she used to live,
A7　　Dm
How his heart was beating. *Chorus*

Dm
Storm and wind and rain and snow,

Nothing would dismay him.
Gm
Even though his mother would
A7　　Dm
Wait at home to flay him.
Gm
Even though his mother would
A7　　Dm
Wait at home to flay him. *Chorus*

OY, DORTN, DORTN
AWAY OUT YONDER

Oy, dor-tn, dor-tn, i-bern vas-er-l, Oy, dor-tn, dor-
A-way out yon-der, far a-cross the wa-ter, A-cross the bridge

tn, i-ber-n brik,_____ Far__ tri-bn hot men mich, in di
that leads__ far a-way,_____ They've__driv-en me a-way, in-to

vay-te-ne len-der, Un ben-kn, benk__ ich noch dir tsu-rik._____
far-off__ coun-tries. And now I long__ for you ev-'ry day._____

Em
Oy, vifil ovntlech, tsuzamen gezesen,

Bm   C D7   G Em
Oy, vifil ovntlech, shpet in di nacht.

Bm Em   D7   Em C
Oy, vifil trerelech mir hobn fargosn,

D7 G   Bm Am B7   E7
Oy, biz mir hobn di libe tsuzamen gebracht.

Em
Oy, dayne oygelech, vi di shvartse karshelech,

Bm   C D7   G Em
Un dayne lipelech, vi rozeve papir.

Bm Em   D7   Em C
In dayne fingerlech, nem tint un feder,

D7 G   Bm Am B7 Em
Oy, shraybn zolstu ofte briv tsu mir.

Em
How many evenings we sat together,

Bm   C D7   G Em
How many evenings, late into the night.

Bm Em   D7   Em C
How many were the tears we shed between us,

D7 G   Bm Am B7 Em
Until our love set everything aright.

Em
Oh, your sweet little eyes, like the blackest cherries,

Bm   C D7   G Em
And your sweet lips, the color of a rose,

Bm   Em   D7   Em C
And your sweet fingertips, I hope that you will use them

D7 G   Bm Am B7   Em
To write me letters often, goodness knows.

BIN ICH MIR GEGANGEN FISHELECH KOYFN
I WENT TO THE MARKET, TO BUY SOME FISH THERE

Bin ich mir ge - gang - en fi - she - lech koy - fn,
I went to the mar - ket to buy some fish there,

Hob ich mir ge - koyft _____ a hecht. _____ Un
And I bought my - self _____ a pike. _____ And

ver es iz shul - dig in un - dzer li - be,
he who is guilt - y, guilt - y of lov - ing,

Der zol oys - geyn vi a lecht! _____
Can't have the thing he would like. _____

Chorus

Day - day - day day - day - day day - day - day day - day - day

Day - day - day day - day - day day - day - day Day.

F   C7   F
Az a kartyozhnik shpilt in kortn,

       C7   F C7
Farshpilt er doch nor zayn gelt.

F   C7   Dm
Ich hob farshpilt mayne yunge yorn,

A7   Dm
Finster iz doch mayn velt. *Chorus*

F   C7. F
On keyn tsigl un on kayn shteyner,

       C7   F   C7
Kon men keyn hoyz nisht moyern.

F   C7 Dm
Ay, s'iz nishto aza mentsh oyf der velt;

A7   Dm
Vos er zol mich nisht badoyern! *Chorus*

F   C7   F
When a gambler plays in his card games,

       C7   F C7
All that he loses is gold.

F   C7   Dm
But all the best years of my life I've lost,

A7   Dm
Now all the world seems so cold. *Chorus*

F   C7   F
If you've no bricks and if you've no stone,

       C7   F   C7
You can't build a house, don't you see?

F   Dm
And there is no one the whole world over,

A7   Dm
Who wouldn't feel sorry for me. *Chorus*

BIZTU MIT MIR BROYGEZ?
ARE YOU ANGRY WITH ME?

Biz - tu mit mir broy - gez, _____ veys ich nit far - vos?
Are you an - gry with me? _____ Why, I can't sup - pose.

Geyst a - rum a gant - sn tog _____ a - rop - ge - lozt di noz.
But you walk a - round all day _____ All with a down - cast nose.

Chorus

Day day day day day day, Day day day day.

Geyst a - rum a gant - sn tog _____ a - rop - ge - lozt di noz.
But you walk a - round all day _____ All with a down - cast nose.

Dm
Un efsher vilstu visn

Az ich hob dich lib?

A7
Lomir beyde ariberforn
Dm
Tsu dem gutn yid. *Chorus*

Dm
Tsu dem gutn yidn,

A pidyen im opgebn.

A7
Vet er far undz got betn
Dm
Far a gut lebn. *Chorus*

*The rabbi.

Dm
And would you like to know

That I still love you?

A7
Let us take a trip together
Dm
To the worthy Jew.* *Chorus*

Dm
For the worthy rabbi

A little gift we'll leave.

A7
He will pray to God for us,
Dm
To help us, I believe. *Chorus*

Dm
Un az mir veln kumen

Tsurik fun gutn yid,
A7
Veln mir beyde ariberforn
Dm
In Zelva oyf dem yarid. *Chorus*

Dm
Dort vel ich dir koyfn

A zeyger mit a keyt,
A7
Un a sheyne groyse shtik
Dm
Zaydns oyf a kleyd. *Chorus*

Dm
To, zayzhe mer nisht broygez

Un greyt oyf gich tsum tish—
A7
Un zets zich mit mir esn,
Dm
Bakumstu fun mir a kush! *Chorus*

Dm
On our homeward journey,

When he's said his prayer,
A7
Let us take a little trip
Dm
To Zelva—to the fair. *Chorus*

Dm
There I will buy for you

A watch and a gold chain,
A7
A bolt of satin for a dress—
Dm
Then we'll go home again. *Chorus*

Dm
So don't be angry with me,

All I ask is this.
A7
Let's sit and eat together, dear,
Dm
And I'll give you a kiss. *Chorus*

OYFN GANIKL
UPON THE DOORSTEP

Sadly

Dm

Ich gey a - roys oy - fn ga - ni - kl, Dos
Up - on the door - step I go out - side, Up -

Gm ... Dm

shte - te - le ba - ku - kn; Ich
on the porch I _____ seat _____ me; Up -

F

gey a - roys oy - fn ga - ni - kl, Dos
on the door - step I go out - side, Up -

Gm ... A7

shte - te - le ba - ku - kn.
on the porch I seat me.

Dm ... Gm

Kumt tsu fli - en a kleyn ___ fey - ge - le, Un
O - ver - head flies a lit - tle bird, And it

Dm ... A

tut zich tsu mir _____ bu - kn;
bows down low to _____ greet me;

Dm ... Gm

Kumt tsu fli - en a kleyn ___ fey - ge - le, Un
O - ver - head flies a lit - tle bird, And it

Dm ... A7 ... Dm

tut zich tsu mir _____ bu - kn.
bows down low to _____ greet _____ me.

Dm
Nisht azoy dos kleyne feygele,
Gm   Dm
Vi dos sheyne flien;
 F
Nisht azoy dos kleyne feygele,
Gm   A7
Vi dos sheyne flien.
   Dm   Gm
Es varft arop mir a kleyn brivele,
Dm   A
Tu ich far dem knien;
   Dm   Gm
Es varft arop mir a kleyn brivele,
  Dm   A7 Dm
Tu ich far dem knien.

    Dm
Ich leyen iber dos ershte shurele:
   Gm   Dm
Der gelibter iz fardorbn.
    F
Ich leyen iber dos ershte shurele:
   Gm   A7
Der gelibter iz fardorbn.
   Dm   Gm
Ich leyen iber dos tsveyte shurele:
   Dm   A
Der gelibter iz geshtorbn!
  Dm   Gm
Ich leyen iber dos tsveyte shurele:
   Dm   A7 Dm
Der gelibter iz geshtorbn!

    Dm
Klaybt tsunoyf ale mayne khavertes,
Gm   Dm
Alemen in eynem;
    F
Klaybt tsunoyf ale mayne khavertes,
Gm   A7
Alemen in eynem.
 Dm   Gm
Ver s'hot nor a libe gefirt,
Dm   A
Zol mir helfn veynen;
Dm   Gm
Ver s'hot nor a libe gefirt,
Dm   A7 Dm
Zol mir helfn veynen.

Dm
The little bird, it flies around,
 Gm   Dm
I hardly can believe it;
    F
The little bird, it flies around,
 Gm   A7
I hardly can believe it.
  Dm   Gm
It casts a letter to the ground,
 Dm   A
I kneel down and retrieve it;
  Dm   Gm
It casts a letter to the ground,
 Dm   A7 Dm
I kneel down and retrieve it.

  Dm
I stand and read the first sentence there:
  Gm   Dm
My true love poison has taken.
  F
I stand and read the first sentence there:
  Gm   A7
My true love poison has taken.
 Dm   Gm
I stand and read the second sentence there:
  Dm   A
He's dead—I am forsaken!
 Dm   Gm
I stand and read the second sentence there:
  Dm   A7 Dm
He's dead—I am forsaken!

  Dm
My girlfriends all please gather round,
   Gm   Dm
There can be no denying;
   F
My girlfriends all please gather round,
   Gm   A7
There can be no denying.
  Dm   Gm
For all who did a true love have
  Dm   A
Will help me in my crying;
  Dm   Gm
For all who did a true love have
  Dm   A7 Dm
Will help me in my crying.

SHVARTSE KARSHELECH
BLACK CHERRIES

Brightly

Shvar - tse kar - she - lech rayst men, _____ Un gri - ne
Ripe black cher - ries are gath - ered, _____ The green are

lozt _____ men shteyn; _____ Shey - ne mey - de - lech nemt men, _____
left on the tree; _____ Pret - ty girls do get cho - sen, _____

_____ Un mi - se lozt _____ men geyn.
For - got - ten are the ug - ly. _____

Chorus

Oy, vey iz tsu mir, _____ Un vey tsu
Oh, woe un - to me, _____ I have shed

may - ne por yor, _____ A li - be hob ich _____ ge -
man - y a tear, _____ I had a true love, _____ you

firt, _____ Fe - li - ke drey fer - tl yor. _____
see, _____ That last - ed al - most a year. _____

D
Vos toyg mir di polke mazurke,

B7   Em
Az tantsn tants ich zi nit.

A7   D
Vos toyg mir dos meydele fun Vurke,

A7   D
Az libn libt zi mich nit. *Chorus*

D
What good is the polka-mazurka?

B7   Em
My heart is not carefree.

A7   D
What good is the maiden from Vurka,

A7   D
When she does not love me? *Chorus*

D
Vos toyg mir der nayer valets—

B7   Em
Az tantsn tants ich im nisht.

A7   D
Vos toyg mir dos meydele fun Shilets,

A7   D
Az libn libt zi mich nisht.   *Chorus*

D
The brand-new waltzes don't thrill me—

B7   Em
Let others go to the ball.

A7   D
The girl from Shilets, she'll kill me,

A7   D
For she doesn't love me at all. *Chorus*

D
Vos toygn mir di lipelech, di sheyne,

B7   Em
Az kushn, kushn zey mich nit?

A7   D
Vos toygn mir di hentelech, di kleyne,

A7   D
Az gletn, gletn zey mich nit? *Chorus*

D
What good do her lips do me?

B7   Em
For I never get a kiss.

A7   D
Her little hands don't come to me,

A7   D
I never get a caress. *Chorus*

Children

Some East European Jewish families stopped off briefly in England on the way to America. This photograph was taken in 1904.

JAMELE

Words by A. LITWIN (1862-1943)
[Pseudonym of S. Hurwitz]

Du vest zayn a g'vir, mayn Ja-me-le, Flaygt mir zin-gen bay mayn
You'll be a rich man, my Ja-me-le, Was the song my moth-er

vi-ge-le, A-le nacht a-mol mayn ma-me-le. Ich ge-
sang to me, As she rocked my cra-dle ten-der-ly. I re-

denk noch haynt ir ni-ge-le. Ich ge-denk noch haynt ir ni-ge-le.
mem-ber well her mel-o-dy. I re-mem-ber well her mel-o-dy.

Am Dm Am		Am Dm Am
Un mekuyom iz gevorn mir		And the prophecy my mother made
Dm Am		Dm Am
Di havtocho fun mayn mamele.		Was fulfilled as the long years rolled by.
Dm Am		Dm Am
Ver hot noch gezayn aza gevir,		Never was there such a wealthy man
F Dm Am		F Dm Am
Aza oysher vi ir Jamele!		As my mother's little Jamele.
Dm E7 Am		Dm E7 Am
Aza oysher vi ir Jamele!		As my mother's little Jamele.
Am Dm Am		Am Dm Am
Shlofn shlof ich oyf a kerbele,		For I sleep upon a bed of straw.
Dm Am		Dm Am
Mach hamoytsi oyf a skorinke,		Say my blessings o'er a crust of bread.
Dm Am		Dm Am
Un l'chayim oyf a sherbele		I've no wine to give a toast to life,
F Dm Am		F Dm Am
Ful mit brunen vasser klorinke.		I drink water from the well instead.
Dm E7 Am		Dm E7 Am
Ful mit brunen vasser klorinke.		I drink water from the well instead.
Am Dm Am		Am Dm Am
Un di kinderlech, dos vaybele,		And the children and my darling wife
Dm Am		Dm Am
Geyen oysgeputst antikele!		Are all dressed in the most stylish things,
Dm Am		Dm Am
Ful mit lates iz dos laybele,		For the jacket is all patched and torn,
F Dm Am		F Dm Am
Arumgegartlt mit a shtrikele.		Held together by a piece of string.
Dm F7 Am		Dm E7 Am
Arumgegartlt mit a shtrikele.		Held together by a piece of string.

UNTER DEM KINDS VIGELE
UNDER BABY'S LITTLE CRIB

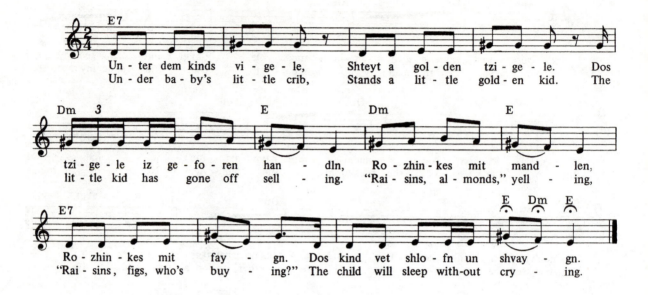

Un - ter dem kinds vi - ge - le, Shteyt a gol - den tzi - ge - le. Dos
Un - der ba - by's lit - tle crib, Stands a lit - tle gold - en kid. The

tzi - ge - le iz ge - fo - ren han - dln, Ro - zhin - kes mit mand - len,
lit - tle kid has gone off sell - ing. "Rai - sins, al - monds," yell - ing,

Ro - zhin - kes mit fay - gn. Dos kind vet shlo - fn un shvay - gn.
"Rai - sins, figs, who's buy - ing?" The child will sleep with - out cry - ing.

E7
Shlof mir, shlof mir in dayn ru,

Mach di koshere eygelach tsu.

Dm   E
Mach zey tsu un mach zey oyf,

Dm   E
Kumt der tate un vekt dich oyf.

E7
Tate, tate, nisht oyfvek!

    E Dm E
Dos kind vet shlofn vayter avek.

E7
Shlofn iz a gute schoyre,

Moishele vet lernen Toyre.

Dm   E
Toyre vet er lernen,

Dm   E
Sforim vet er shraybn.

E7
A guter un a frumer,

    E Dm E
Vet er m'yertseshem b l a y b n.

E7
Go to sleep in sweet repose,

Soon your lovely eyes will close.

Dm   E
Close them tight, then open wide,

Dm   E
Now your papa's by your side.

E7
Papa, papa, softly creep!

    E Dm E
The baby's going to fall asleep.

E7
Sleep is what the baby needs,

Moishele will do great deeds.

Dm   E
He will study holy writ,

Dm   E
Torah, he will master it.

E7
Full of good and piety,

    E Dm E
Will he, God willing, ever be.

SHLOF, MAYN FEYGELE
SLEEP, MY LITTLE BIRD

Shlof, mayn fey - ge - le, mach tsu dayn ey - ge - le,
Sleep, my lit - tle bird, do not say a word,

Ay - lu - lu - lu. Shlof ge - shmok, mayn kind,
Ay - lu - lu - lu. Sleep se - cure, my dear,

shlof un zay ge - zunt, Ay - lu - lu - lu -
sleep and have no fear, Ay - lu - lu - lu -

lu. Shlof un cho - lem zis, fun der velt ge - nis,
lu. May your dreams be sweet, and your joy com - plete,

Ay - lu - lu - lu. Kol - z'man du bist yung,
Ay - lu - lu - lu. While you are still young,

ken - stu shlu - fen gring, lach - en fun als - ding, Ay lu lu.
none can do you wrong, just en - joy my song, Ay lu lu.

OYFN PRIPETSHOK
ON THE HEARTH

Mark Warshawsky (1848–1907) has been called the Yiddish Robert Burns. Comparing him also to Woody Guthrie would not be far from the truth either. In his lifetime, as also happened with the Scottish bard and the Okie balladeer, the songs of Mark Warshawsky came to be regarded as genuine folk songs. He practiced law in Kiev—not too successfully—while composing for his own pleasure, and the pleasure of his friends, songs mirroring Russian-Jewish life as he knew it. However, it was not until 1899 that he began to achieve widespread recognition for his works. In that year the writer Sholem Aleichem first heard Warshawsky's songs. He immediately recognized their true worth and a fast friendship grew between the two men. They frequently performed together, Sholem Aleichem reading from his works and Warshawsky singing his. In 1900 a first edition of his *Yidishe Folkslider* (*Yiddish Folk Songs*), published in Kiev, sold out. Warshawsky dreamed of going to America and performing his material there, but he never did. In 1918, Sholem Aleichem brought out the second edition of *Yidishe Folkslider* in New York.

By **MARK WARSHAWSKY**

Em   Am   B7 Em
Lernt kinder, mit groys cheyshek,
  G   D7 G
Azoy zog ich aych on;
Am   Em
Ver s'vet gicher fun aych kenen "Ivre,"
B7   Em (E7)*
Der bakumt a fon.   *Chorus*   2

Em   Am   B7 Em
Lernt kinder, hot nit moyre,
  G   D7 G
Yeder onhoyb iz shver;
Am   Em
Gliklech iz der vos lernt Toyre,
  B7   Em (E7)
Tsi darf der mentsh noch mer? *Chorus*   2

Em   Am B7 Em
Ir vet, kinder, elter vern,
  G   D7   G
Vet ir aleyn farshteyn,
Am   Em
Vifil in di oysyes lign trern,
B7   Em (E7)
Un vifil geveyn. *Chorus*   2

Em   Am B7 Em
Az ir vet, kinder dem goles shlepn,
  G   D7 G
Oysgemutshet zayn,
Am   Em
Zolt ir fun di oysyes koyech shepn,
B7   Em (E7)
Kukt in zey arayn! *Chorus*   2

Em   Am   B7 Em
Learn your lessons well, with great interest,
  G   D7 G
That is what I say.
Am   Em
He who gets to know his Hebrew best of all
B7   Em (E7)*
Wins a prize today. *Chorus*   2

Em   Am   B7 Em
Learn your lessons well, do not be afraid,
  G   D7   G
Hardest is the start.
Am   Em
Happy is the man who learns the Torah well,
B7   Em (E7)
Clasps it to his heart. *Chorus*   2

Em   Am   B7 Em
Children, you will learn, when you're older,
  G   D7 G
You'll know all too well,
Am   Em
Of the tears that lie in every letter—
B7   Em (E7)
More than tongue can tell. *Chorus*   2

Em   Am   B7 Em
If it happens that you should be exiled,
  G   D7   G
Suffering great pain,
Am   Em
From these letters may you gain your strength;
B7   Em (E7)
Look at them again. *Chorus*   2

Repeat first verse.

*(E7): for repeats

SHLOF, MAYN KIND
SLEEP, MY CHILD

Even if you were to tell me eighteen times over: *Aeoliski, Doriski, Miksolidski* and other such high-sounding musical terms of "the language of the spheres," what can we simple little folk know? At the mere sound of such words we prick up our ears, thinking in the meantime: Now there's a fellow for you! Although, if you look at it in another way, we can say something about music too. After all, music is a Jewish matter, you know, and which Jew does not understand about singing? —*Sholem Aleichem*

Words by **SHOLEM ALEICHEM**
Music by **DAVID KOVANOVSKI**

Shlof, mayn kind, mayn treyst mayn shey - ner, Shlof - zhe zu - ne -
Sleep, my child, my great - est plea - sure, Sleep my lit - tle

nyu. Shlof, mayn le - bn, mayn ka - dish ey - ner, Shlof - zhe, lyu - lyu -
son, Sleep, my life and my dear - est trea - sure, Sleep, my dar - ling —

lyu. Shlof, mayn le - bn, mayn ka - dish ey - ner, Shlof - zhe, lyu - lyu - lyu.
one. Sleep, my life and my dear - est trea - sure, Sleep, my dar - ling —— one.

E
Bay dayn vigl zitst dayn mame,
C#m   E
Zingt a lid un veynt.
              B7
Du vest amol farshteyn mistame,
Em Edim B7
Vos zi hot gemeynt.

E   A   E
Du vest amol farshteyn mistame,
B7   E
Vos zi hot gemeynt.

E
In Amerike iz der tate,
C#m   E
Dayner, zunyenyu.
              B7
Du bizt noch a kind l'es ate,
  Em   Edim B7
Shlof-zhe, lyu-lyu-lyu.
E   A   E
Du bizt noch a kind l'es ate,
B7   E
Shlof-zhe, lyu-lyu-lyu.

E
By your cradle sits your mother,
C#m   E
Sings a song and cries.
              B7
One day you will know the reason
Em Edim B7
For those tear-filled eyes.

E   A   E
One day you will know the reason
B7   E
For those tear-filled eyes.

E
In America is father,
C#m   E
Far across the sea.
              B7
You are still a little baby—
  Em   Edim B7
Sleep, then peacefullly.
E   A   E
You are still a little baby—
B7   E
Sleep, then, peacefully.

E
In Amerike iz far yedn,
C#m   E
Zogt men, gor a glik.

      B7
Un far yedn, a gan-eydn,
Em   Edim B7
Gor epes an antik.
   E   A   E
Un far yedn, a gan-eydn,

B7   E
Gor epes an antik.

     E
Dortn est men in der vochn
C#m   E
Chale, zunyenyu.

        B7
Yaychelech vel ich dir kochn,
   Em   Edim B7
Shlof-zhe, lyu-lyu-lyu.
   E   A   E
Yaychelech vel ich dir kochn,

   B7   E
Shlof-zhe, lyu-lyu-lyu.

     E
Er vet shikn tsvantsig doler,
C#m   E
Zayn portret dertsu,

        B7
Un vet nemen, lebn zol er!
Em Edim B7
Undz ahintsutsu.
   E   A   E
Un vet nemen, lebn zol er!

   B7   E
Undz ahintsutsu.

     E
Er vet chapn undz un kushn,
C#m   E
Tantsn nor far freyd!

        B7
Ich vel kvaln trern gisn,
   Em   Edim B7
Veynen shtilerheyt.
   E   A   E
Ich vel kvaln trern gisn,

   B7   E
Veynen shtilerheyt.

     E
Biz es kumt dos gute kvitl,
C#m   E
Shlof-zhe, zunynenyu.

        B7
Shlofn iz a tayer mitl,
   Em   Edim B7
Shlof-zhe, lyu-lyu-lyu.
     E   A   E
Shlofn iz a tayer mitl,

   B7   E
Shlof-zhe, lyu-lyu-lyu.

E
In America, they tell me,
C#m   E
There is happiness.

        B7
Paradise on earth is waiting—
Em Edim B7
End to all distress.
   E   A   E
Paradise on earth is waiting—

B7   E
End to all distress.

     E
There the people eat on weekdays
C#m   E
Chale,* little son.

        B7
I will cook you lots of goodies,
Em   Edim B7
Sleep, my precious one.
E   A   E
I will cook you lots of goodies,

   B7   E
Sleep, my precious one.

E
He will send us twenty dollars,
C#m   E
And his portrait, too.

        B7
And he'll take us, long life to him!
Em   Edim B7
To build life anew.
     E   A   E
And he'll take us, long life to him!

B7   E
To build life anew.

     E
He'll embrace us and he'll kiss us,
C#m   E
We will dance for joy.

             B7
Tears will pour down silently—
   Em   Edim B7
Sleep, my little boy.
   E   A   E
Tears will pour down silently—

B7   E
Sleep, my little boy.

     E
Till he sends the precious ticket,
C#m   E
Sleep, my little son.

             B7
Sleeping makes you strong and healthy,
   Em   Edim   B7
Sleep, my precious one.
   E   A   E
Sleeping makes you strong and healthy,

B7   E
Sleep, my precious one.

*Chale—sweet white bread usually eaten on the Sabbath and holidays.

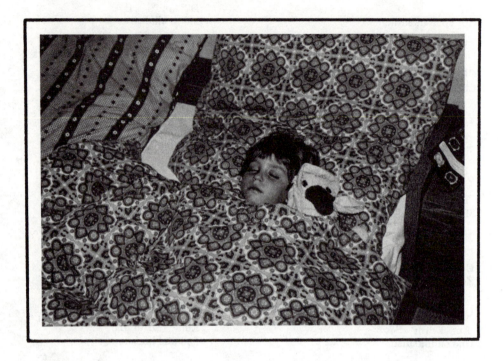

VIGNDIG A FREMD KIND

ROCKING SOMEONE ELSE'S CHILD
(The Baby-Sitter's Complaint)

Zolst a-zoy le-bn Un zayn ge-zint, Vi ich _ vel dir zi-tsn Un vi-gn s'kind.
You can't im-ag-ine, It drives me wild, To sit _ here all day And to rock this child.

Chorus

Ay - lyu - lyu, Sha - sha - sha! Dayn ma-me-shi z'ge-gan-gen In mark a - rayn.
Hush - a - bye, Don't you cry! Your ma-ma she has gone out, Some food to buy.

Ay - lyu - lyu, Shlof, mayn kind, Di ma-me-shi vet ku - men Gich un g'shvind.
Hush - a - bye, Sleep, my child; Your ma-ma will re-turn In just a while.

Dm
Zolst azoy lebn,

F
S'geyt mir derinen!

C7   A7
Dayn mameshi z'gegangen

Dm
In mark arayn fardinen. *Chorus*

Dm
I can't take it,

F
It's just not fair—

C7   A7
Your mother has gone off

Dm
To work somewhere. *Chorus*

Dm
Andere meydelech

F
Tantsen un shpringen,

C7   A7
Un ich muzn' kind

Dm
Vign un zingen! *Chorus*

Dm
Other young girls

F
Dance and play,

C7   A7
While here by the cradle

Dm
I must stay. *Chorus*

Dm
Andere meydelech

F
Tsukerkelech nashn,

C7   A7
Un ich muzn's kind

Dm
Vindelech vashn! *Chorus*

Dm
Other young girls

F
Candies are *noshing,**

C7   A7
And I've got a pile of

Dm
Diapers for washing. *Chorus*

*noshing—snacking, nibbling.

51

ROZHINKES MIT MANDLEN
RAISINS AND ALMONDS

By **ABRAHAM GOLDFADEN**
(1840-1906)

In dem beys ha-mik-dash in a vin - kl chey-der, Zitst di al-
In the ho-ly Tem-ple, all a-lone in a cor-ner, Sits the old

mo-ne bas-tsi-oyn a - leyn. Ir ben-yo-chi-dl i-de-le vigt zi ke-
wid-ow, the Daugh-ter of Zion. And she rocks her young son, ly-ing there in the

sey-der, Un zingt im tsum shlo-fn a li-de-le sheyn: Un-tern yi-de-le's
cra-dle, And sings him to sleep with this sweet lul-la-by: 'Neath the cra-dle of

vi-ge-le, _____ Shteyt a klor-vays _____ tsi-ge-le. _____ Dos
my _____ young _____ son, _____ Stands a goat, yes, a pure _____ white _____ one. _____ The

tsi-ge-le iz ge-fo-rn han-dlen, _____ Dos vet zayn dayn ba-
lit-tle goat has been fat-ed to wan-der, _____ That will be your fate,

ruf. _____ Ro-zhin-kes _____ mit man-dlen, _____
too. _____ Rai-sins sweet _____ and al-monds, _____

Shlof-zhe, yi-de-le, shlof, _____ Shlof-zhe, yi-de-le, shlof. _____
Sleep then, my lit-tle Jew, _____ Sleep then, my lit-tle Jew. _____

DRAY YINGELECH
THREE LITTLE BOYS

Words by **I. GOYCHBERG**
Music by **M. GELBART**

Di ma - me hot dray yin - ge - lech, Dray yin - ge - lech ge - hat, Mit
My ma - ma had three lit - tle boys, Three lit - tle boys had she, With

vey - che, roy - te be - ke - lech, Vi tsar - ter sa - met glat. Hot eyns ge - hey - sn
ten - der, ros - y lit - tle cheeks, All smooth and sa - tin - y. The first, he was called

Be - re - le, Dos tsvey - te, Cha - yim Shme - re - le, Dos dri - te hot ge - hey - sn— Men
Be - re - le, The sec - ond, Cha - yim Shme - re - le, The third one he just called for A

zol im koy - fn shich. Ich hob aych op - ge - nart, Ich hob ge - vust ir
brand-new pair of shoes. You real - ly want to know Who the third one can

vart. Dos dri - te kley - ne yin - ge - le— Dos dri - te, dos bin ich.
be? It real - ly is not hard to guess—That lit - tle boy is me.

54

```
     C   G7      C  G7
Di mame hot dray niselech
     C   G7      C  G7
Fun dem yarid gebracht.
     C   G7 C  G7
Dray gute, fete niselech,
     C  G7     C
Dray niselch a pracht.

        Am         Em
    Iz eyns geven far Berelen,
        Am             Em
    Un eyns far Chayim-Shmerelen,
        G7         C    A7
    Un gor dos beste nisl—
        Dm  G7     C
    Hot zi gelozt far zich.

    Ir vundert zich abisl,
         F            C
    Far vos nit mir keyn nisl?
         F          C
    Vayl nisn, nisn, nisele,
         G7        C
    Dos drite dos bin ich.
```

```
     C   G7      C   G7
My mama once went to the fair
         C       G7     C   G7
And brought three nuts back home.
         C    G7   C   G7
Three plump, delicious little nuts,
         C       G7       C
They caused our mouths to foam.

        Am         Em
    Well, one it was for Berele,
        Am              Em
    And one for Chayim Shmerele,
        G7          C       A7
    But then the very best one—
        Dm   G7    C
    She saved it for herself.

    You'd like to know the reason,
         F             C
    No nut for number-three son.
         F          C
    It really is a funny game—
         G7         C
    For Nisele's* my name.
```

*A play on words: *nisele* is the word for nut as well as a boy's name.

BAY DEM SHTETL SHTEYT A SHTIBL
IN THE VILLAGE THERE'S A CABIN

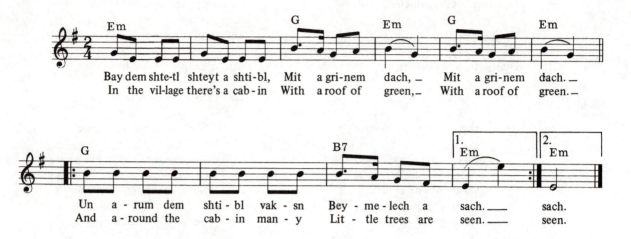

Bay dem shte-tl shteyt a shti-bl, Mit a gri-nem dach, — Mit a gri-nem dach. —
In the vil-lage there's a cab-in With a roof of green, — With a roof of green. —

Un a-rum dem shti-bl vak-sn Bey-me-lech a sach. —— sach.
And a-round the cab-in man-y Lit-tle trees are seen. —— seen.

Em
Un der tate mit der mame,
G   Em
Chanele mit mir,
G   Em
Chanele mit mir,
G
Shoyn a lange tsayt ineynim
B7   Em
Voynen ale fir.   2

Em
With my father and my mother,
G   Em
Chanele and me,
G   Em
Chanele and me,
G
We've been living all together—
B7   Em
Our family.   2

Em
Un der tate, horevet, horevet,
G   Em
Ale yorn zayne,
G   Em
Ale yorn zayne.
G
Un er koyft undz, un er brengt undz,
B7   Em
Zachn sheyne, fayne.   2

Em
How my father struggles, struggles,
G   Em
Year after year,
G   Em
Year after year.
G
But he buys us and he brings us
B7   Em
Pretty things and dear.   2

Em
Brengt a hintele vos se havket,

G   Em
Mitn nomen Tsutsik,

G   Em
Mitn nomen Tsutsik.

 G
Brengt a ferdl vos se hirzhet,

B7   Em
Mitn nomen Mutsik.   ] 2

Em
Once he bought a barking puppy,

G   Em
And we called him Tsutsik,

G   Em
And we called him Tsutsik.

G
Then he brought a neighing pony,

B7   Em
And we named him Mutsik.   ] 2

Em
Brengt a gendzele mit a langn haldz,

G   Em
Federlech vays vi shney,

G   Em
Federlech vays vi shney.

 G
Brengt a hun vos kvoket, kvoket,

B7   Em
Biz zi leygt an ey!   ] 2

Em
Brought a long-necked goose one day,

G   Em
Feathers white as snow,

G   Em
Feathers white as snow.

G
And a hen that cackled, cackled,

B7   Em
Laid an egg, you know!   ] 2

Em
Nemt di mame ot di eye,

G   Em
Ay, iz dos a moyfes!

G   Em
Ay, iz dos a moyfes!

 G
Zetst zi oyf oyf zey a kvoke:

B7   Em
Hobn mir naye oyfes!   ] 2

Em
Mama gathered up the eggs—

G   Em
This is very tricky.

G   Em
This is very tricky.

G
Put them underneath the hen

B7   Em
And out came chicky-chicky!   ] 2

O, IR KLEYNE LICHTELECH
OH, YOU LITTLE CANDLE LIGHTS
A Song for Chanukah

Words by **MORRIS ROSENFELD**

O, ir kley - ne lich - te - lech, Ir der - tseylt ge -
Oh, you lit - tle can - dle - lights, Burn - ing for eight

shich - te - lech, May - se - lech on a tsol.
days and nights, Won - der - ful tales you tell.

Ir der - tselyt fun blu - ti - keyt, Ber - ye - shaft un mu - ti -
Bat - tles fought 'gainst slav - er - y. Skill and blood and brav - er -

1.
keyt, Vun - der fun a - mol.
y, Long a - go be - fell.

2.
fun a - mol.
go be - fell.

Am
Ven ich ze aych finklendik,

Dm   Am
Kumt a cholem pintlendik,

    Em   B7   Em   E7
Ret an alter troym.

A7   Dm
Yid, du host gekrigt amol,

G7   C
Yid, du host gezigt amol,

    E7   Am   E7
Ach, dos gloybt zich koym.

A7   Dm
Yid, du host gekrigt amol,

G7   C
Yid, du host gezigt amol,

    E7   Am
Ach, dos gloybt zich koym.

Am
When your twinkling lights I see,

Dm   Am
Then a dream appears to me,

    Em   B7   Em   E7
Dream of long ago.

A7   Dm
Jew, in battles you did stand,

G7   C
Jew, with vict'ries in your hand,

    E7   Am   E7
Where did those times go?

A7   Dm
Jew, in battles you did stand,

G7   C
Jew, with vict'ries in you hand,

    E7   Am
Where did those times go?

HULYET, HULYET, KINDERLECH
PLAY, MY DEAREST LITTLE ONES

Shpilt aych li - be kin - der - lech, Der fri - ling shoyn ba - gint, Der
Play, my dear - est lit - tle ones, For spring is here at last, For

fri - ling shoyn ba - gint. Oy, vi ich bin, kin - der - lach, Me - ka - ne aych a __
spring is here at last. As for me, my lit - tle chil - dren, All my springs are __

tsint. Oy, vi ich bin, kin - der - lech, Me - ka - ne aych a - tsint.
past. As for me, my lit - tle __ chil - dren, All my springs are past.

Chorus

Hul - yet, hul - yet, __ kin - der - lech, Kol - zman ir zeyt noch ying,
Have a good time, __ lit - tle ones, While your youth is still here,

Vayl fun fri - ling biz tsum vin - ter Iz a kats - en - shpring.
For from spring to win - ter - time Is short - er than a year.

Am Shpilt aych, libe kinderlech,	Am Play, my dearest little ones,
Dm Am Farzoymt keyn oygenblik,	Dm Am And do not waste your time,
F G7 C A7 Farzoymt keyn oygenblik.	F G7 C A7 And do not waste your time.
Dm Am Nemt mich oych arayn in shpil,	Dm Am Let me join you in your game—
F E A7 Fargint mir oych dos glik?	F E A7 Can all your joy be mine?
Dm Am Nemt mich oych arayn in shpil,	Dm Am Let me join you in your game--
E7 Am Fargint mir oych dos glik? *Chorus*	E7 Am Can all your joy be mine? *Chorus*

Am
Kukt nisht oyf mayn groyen kop,

Dm   Am
Tsi shtert dos aych in shpil?

 F G7 C A7
Tsi shtert dos aych in shpil?

Dm   Am
Mayn neshome iz noch yung,

 F   E A7
Vi ts'rik mit yorn fil.

Dm   Am
Mayn neshome iz noch yung,

   E7 Am
Vi ts'rik mit yorn fil. *Chorus*

Am
Mayn neshome iz noch yung,

 Dm   Am
Un geyt fun benkshaft oys,

 F G7   C A7
Un geyt fun benkshaft oys.

Dm Am
Ach, vi gern vilt zich ir

 F   E A7
Fun altn guf aroys.

Dm   Am
Ach, vi gern vilt zich ir

   E7 Am
Fun altn guf aroys. *Chorus*

Am
Shpilt aych, libe kinderlech,

 Dm   Am
Farzoymt keyn oygenblik,

  F G7 C A7
Farzoymt keyn oygenblik.

Dm   Am
Vayl der friling ekt zich bald,

 F   E A7
Mit im dos hechste glik.

Dm   Am
Vayl der friling ekt zich bald,

    E7 Am
Mit im dos hechste glik. *Chorus*

Am
Don't look at my graying head,

 Dm   Am
Does it disturb your fun?

   F G7   C A7
Does it disturb your fun?

Dm   Am
For my soul is still as young

 F   E A7
As 'twas in years bygone.

Dm   Am
For my soul is still as young

    E7 Am
As 'twas in years bygone. *Chorus*

Am
Yes, my soul, it is still young,

 Dm   Am
And longingly does pine,

  F G7   C A7
And longingly does pine.

Dm   Am
Oh, how gladly would it rise up,

 F   E A7
And go back in time.

Dm   Am
Oh, how gladly would it rise up,

   E7 Am
And go back in time. *Chorus*

Am
Play, my dearest little ones,

 Dm   Am
And do not waste your time,

  F G7   C A7
And do not waste your time.

Dm   Am
For the springtime will soon end—

  F   E A7
With it your joy sublime.

Dm   Am
For the springtime will soon end—

    E7 Am
With it your joy sublime. *Chorus*

BIROBIZHANER VIGLID
BIROBIDJAN LULLABY

Words by **ITZIK FEFFER**
Music by **R. BOYARSKAYA**

See the note for "Birobidjan," page 85.

Shlof mayn kind, far mach di oy gn, Tunk ler ver n
Sleep, my child, and close your eyes, The hills are grow ing

berg. S'iz an od ler durch ge floy gn, Zayn zol stu vi er.
dim. High a bove an ea gle flies by, May you be like him.

S'iz an od ler durch ge floy gn, Zayn zol stu vi er.
High a bove an ea gle flies by May you be like him.

E
S'flegt dayn tate oyf di vegn,

Shlepn dem geveyn.
    Am
Oyf Amurer sheyne vegn,
      E
Boyen mir a heym.

Oyf Amurer sheyne vegn,

Dm   E
Boyen mir a heym.

E
Once upon a time your father

Sorrowfully did roam.
    Am
Now upon the Amur's banks
      E
We all shall build a home.

Now upon the Amur's banks

Dm   E
We all shall build a home.

E
Un vi er zolstu zich hoybn,

Zayn mit volkns glaych.
　　　Am
Durch di ovntdike shoybn,
　　　　　E
Kukt der Biro taych.

Durch di ovntdike shoybn,
　Dm　　　　E
Kukt der Biro taych.

E
And like him, may you, too, rise up,

Like the clouds on high.
　　　　　　　　Am
Through the window see the
　　　　　　　　　　E
Bira River flowing by.

Through the window see the
　　　　Dm　　　E
Bira River flowing by.

E
Un far der heym veln mir zich shlogn,

Biz'n letstn blut.
　　　　　Am
S'hoybt di zun shoyn on tsu togn,
　　　　　　E
Shlof, mayn kind, barut.

S'hoybt di zun shoyn on tsu togn,
　　Dm　　　　E
Shlof, mayn kind, barut.

E
For this home we'll fight if need be,

Though it cost us dear.
　　　　　　Am
Now the dawn is breaking slowly,
　　　　　　　　E
Sleep, child, have no fear.

Now the dawn is breaking slowly,
　　Dm　　　　　E
Sleep, child, have no fear.

Postmarks from 1935, 1947, and 1955 from Birobidzhan illustrating the downgrading and eventual disappearance of Yiddish in favor of Russian.

A FIDLER
A FIDDLER

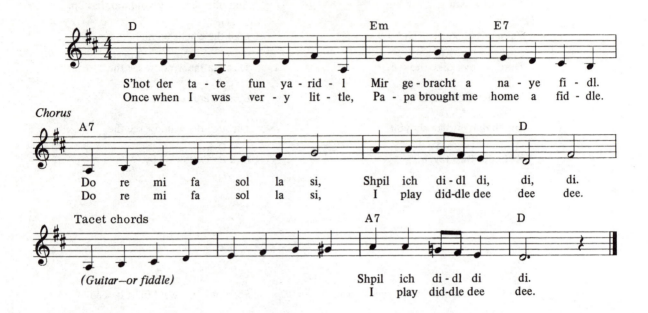

S'hot der ta - te fun ya - rid - l Mir ge - bracht a na - ye fi - dl.
Once when I was ver - y lit - tle, Pa - pa brought me home a fid - dle.

Chorus

Do re mi fa sol la si, Shpil ich di - dl di, di, di.
Do re mi fa sol la si, I play did - dle dee dee dee.

Tacet chords

(Guitar—or fiddle)

Shpil ich di - dl di di.
I play did-dle dee dee.

D
Ch'halt dos kepl ongeboygen,

Em   E7
Un farglots di beyde oygn.   *Chorus*

D
Rechtn fus faroys a bisl,

Em   E7
Klap dem takt tsu mitn fisl.   *Chorus*

D
Kvelt un vundert zich di mame,

Em   E7
"Kenst doch azoy gut di game!"   *Chorus*

D
Hold my head at the right angle,

Em   E7
Do not let the fiddle dangle.   *Chorus*

D
With my right foot out I must stand,

Em   E7
Counting, tapping, "One-and, two-and."   *Chorus*

D
Mama can't keep herself steady,

Em   E7
"See, he knows the scale already!"   *Chorus*

Lechayim!

IN DER KUZNYE
IN THE SMITHY

By SHMUEL AYCHEL
(1886-1943)

In der kuz-nye bay dem fay - er, Shteyt der shmi-der un er shmidt. Er klapt dos ay - zn, fun-ken fay-er fli - en,
In the smith-y by the fi - re, Stands the black-smith tall and strong. He strikes the an - vil, sparks of fire scat - ter,

Un er zingt der-bay a lid. Er klapt dos lid.
And he sings a lust-y song. He strikes the song.

C   G C
Fun der frayhayt vos vet kumen,
       G7   C G7
Zingt er mutik, zingt er heys;
   Am
Un er shpirt nit vi es gist zich
G7   C G7
Fun zayn ponim taychn shveys.
   Am
Un er shpirt nit vi es gist zich
G7   C
Fun zayn ponim taychn shveys.

C   G C
Sings of freedom that is coming,
         G7   C G7
And his brave song rocks the place.
   Am
But he takes no notice of the streams
G7   C G7
Of perspiration on his face.
   Am
But he takes no notice of the streams
G7   C
Of perspiration on his face.

```
        C              G   C
Shtark batsoybert fun der frayhayt,

           G7      C    G7
Zingt er vayter un es klingt,

          Am
Nor der hamer klapt noch hecher

G7                 C    G7
Un er hert nit vos er zingt.

          Am
Nor der hamer klapt noch hecher

G7                    C
Un er hert nit vos er zingt.


         C              G   C
Fun der erd batsirt mit blumen

            G7      C    G7
Zingt er vayter in zayn lid;

         Am
Opgekilt iz shoyn dos ayzn

G7                 C    G7
Un er klapt un vert nit mid.

         Am
Opgekilt iz shoyn dos ayzn

G7                    C
Un er klapt un vert nit mid.
```

```
        C                  G   C
Thoughts of freedom are enchanting;

              G7      C    G7
He keeps singing, and it rings.

           Am
But the hammer, it beats stronger,

G7                      C    G7
And he hears not what he sings.

           Am
But the hammer, it beats stronger,

G7                         C
And he hears not what he sings.


        C                    G   C
Of the earth bedecked with flowers,

             G7      C    G7
He continues on, inspired.

           Am
Now his anvil's growing cooler,

G7                     C    G7
Still he strikes and is not tired.

           Am
Now his anvil's growing cooler,

G7                     C
Still he strikes and is not tired.
```

DI BORD
THE BEARD

With spirit

Az Tshi - pe - Tray - ne iz in shtub a - rayn - ge - ku - men,
When Tshi - pe - Tray - ne came home the oth - er eve - ning,

Hot zi ir ey - ge - nem man nit der - kent. Di gan - tshitsh - ke
She did not re - cog - nize her own hus - band, For he was clean -

bord a - run - ter ge - nu - men, Hot zi ge - macht a
shav - en, his beard was miss - ing, Her scream of shock was

yo - mer - lech ge - vald. Di bord, di bord, di
heard through - out the land. The beard, the beard, the

bord zol mir zayn, Di bord, di bord, in ta - tn a -
beard let it be, The beard, the beard for dear old dad -

rayn! Di bord, di bord, di bord zol mir
dy! The beard, the beard, the beard let it

zayn, __ Di bord, __ di bord, in ta - tn a - rayn!
be, __ The beard, __ the beard for dear old dad - dy!

```
  C                A7      Dm
Tsi iz dos a man, tsi iz dos a bocher,
  G7                              C
Tsi iz dos a nekeyve, tsi iz dos a zocher,
                                    F
Tsi zol ich dos trachtn, tsi zol ich dos klern,
  G7
Az mayn frumer man zol zich di bord gor

        C
   opshern? Chorus
```

```
  C                A7      Dm
Tsi hot dir di bord geton a roe?
  G7                          C
Tsi hot zi dir gekost a spetsyele hotsoe?
                          F
Tsi hot zi fun dir gor gemont esn?
  G7                              C
Oy gevald geshrign, ich ken dos nit fargesn! Chorus
```

```
     C                A7      Dm
Nechtn bay nacht iz mir gekumen tsu cholem
  G7                      C
Di gantshitshke bord olehasholem;
                F
A hor ahin un a hor aher—
  G7                        C
Un lebn der bord iz gelegn a sher. Chorus
```

```
  C                A7      Dm
Now, is this a man, or a boy, maybe?
  G7                              C
Now, is this a woman—say what can it be?
                                    F
And should I believe it—it really is weird,
  G7
That my good old man should shave off

        C
   his beard. Chorus
```

```
  C                A7      Dm
Or did you think that the beard was a vice?
  G7                          C
Or maybe it cost you a special price?
                                    F
Or did it demand from you something to eat?
  G7                              C
I'll never forget it! she screamed in great heat. Chorus
```

```
  C                A7      Dm
The other night a dream came to me
  G7                          C
May it rest in peace—the beard I did see
                          F
A hair over there and a hair over here,
  G7                              C
And alongside the beard there lay the shears. Chorus
```

DI MECHUTONIM GEYEN
THE INLAWS ARE ARRIVING

By MARK WARSHAWSKY

Lively

Di me-chu-to-nim gey-en, kin-der,
Now all the in-laws are ar-riv-ing,

Lo-mir zich frey-en— Shat nor, shat! Der cho-sn iz gor a
Let's all be hap-py— Come and see! The bride-groom is just a

vun-der, Shpilt a li-de-le dem cho-sns tsad,
won-der, Play a song just for his fam-i-ly,

Chorus

Ay-ay, ay-ay-ay, ay-ay, ay___ ay___ ay!

Ay-ay-ay, ay-ay-ay, ay-ay-ay-ay, ay-ay-ay!

Em
Dem chosns shvester Freydl,

C B7
Zi dreyt zich vi a dreydl—shat nor, shat!

Em
Nemt zi arayn in redl

B
Un shpilt a lidele dem chosns tsad. *Chorus*

Em
The bridegroom's sister, Freydl,

C B7
Like a top spins—come and see!

Em
Take her into the circle

B
And play a song for his family. *Chorus*

Em
Ot geyt der feter Mindik,

C B7
Vos hobn mir gezindikt—shat nor, shat!

Em
Er blozt zich vi an indik,

B
Shpilt a lidele dem chosns tsad. *Chorus*

Em
Now, here comes Uncle Mindik,

C B7
Have we ever wronged him?--come and see!

Em
He's puffed up like a turkey;

B
Play a song just for his family. *Chorus*

Em
Dort geyt Elye dem chosns feter,

C   B7
Dem baychl glet er—shat nor, shat!

Em
Er iz feter fun ale feters,

B
Shpilt a lidele dem chosns tsad. *Chorus*

Em
Here come Elye, the bridegroom's uncle,

C   B7
He pats his belly—come and see!

Em
He's fatter than all others;

B
Play a song just for his family. *Chorus*

Hirsh Mindlin (seated far left) with his family. This picture was sent from Russia to his brother in America in 1928.

DI SOCHE
THE PLOW

Elyokum Zunser was a well-known *badchn* (an entertainer who improvised songs at weddings). In this song, written in 1888, he celebrates the settlement of Palestine by Russian Jews.

By **ELYOKUM ZUNSER**
(1840-1915)

In so - che Ligt di ma - zl - bro - che, Der va - rer glik fun le - bn,
The plow Will show the peo - ple how We can have the joy of liv - ing,

Kayn zach mir nit felt! Es kumt der fri - mor - gn, Ich darf nit lay - en,
I don't need a thing! Ban-ished is all sor - row, I need not lend or

bor - gn, Der moy - ech darf nit zor - gn Oyf tog— he - tso - es,
bor - row, Or wor - ry 'bout to - mor - row; No prob - lems does it

gelt. S'iz on - ge - greyt oyf vin - ter A za - sik a ge -
bring. I've tak - en win - ter's mea - sure, My store - house holds a

zun - ter, Ich zey un shnayd gants mun - ter — Fray in go - tes velt.
trea - sure, I sow and reap with plea - sure; I live like a king.

```
    Am
Fun raychn

Dm              Am
Ver ken zich tsu mir glaychn?

Dm              E
Ver lebt ruik, gliklech

    F    G      C   E7
Vi ich, poyer in feld?

Am              C
Git nor got dem regn,

Dm              Am
Fil ich glik un zegn,

    Dm              Am E
Ich fir shoyn snopes vegn,

    F   Dm      E
Kheyune far der velt.

Am              C
Ich tu layt dernern,

    Dm              Am
Marklayt un shpaychlern,

Dm              Am E
Shifers, komisyonern—

    Am      E      Am
Un kosher iz mayn gelt.
```

```
    Am
My treasure,

Dm              Am
I'm rich beyond measure.

        Dm              E
Who lives as calmly, happily

    F    G      C   E7
As I, plowing the land?

    Am              C
As long as crops are growing,

    Dm              Am
With happiness I'm glowing,

    Dm              Am E
To harvest I am going—

    F       Dm      E
Enough for all at hand.

Am              C
I'm the food supplier,

    Dm              Am
Marketer and buyer.

Dm              Am E
I can hire, fire,

    Am      E      Am
And the feeling's grand.
```

SHPRAYZ ICH MIR
WALKING DOWN THE HIGHWAY

Words by S. KAHN
Music by E. TEITELBAUM

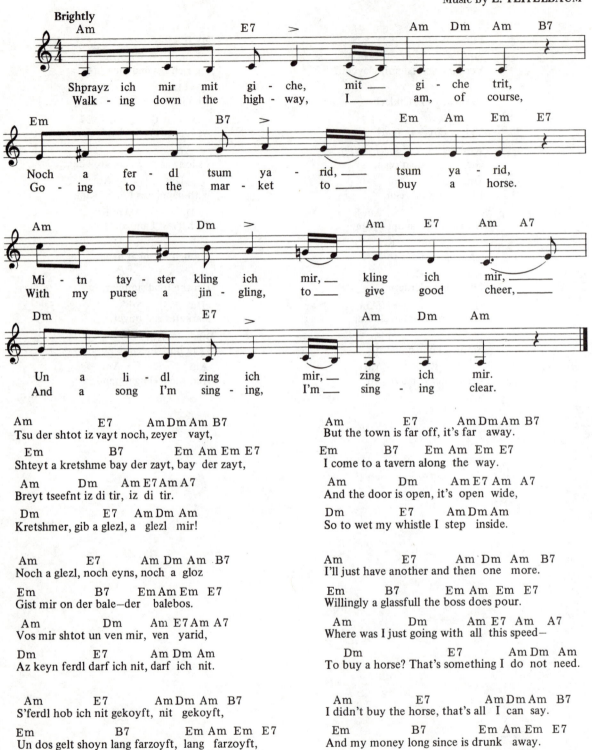

Brightly

Shprayz ich mir mit gi-che, mit gi-che trit,
Walk-ing down the high-way, I am, of course,

Noch a fer-dl tsum ya-rid, tsum ya-rid,
Go-ing to the mar-ket to buy a horse.

Mi-tn tay-ster kling ich mir, kling ich mir,
With my purse a jin-gling, to give good cheer,

Un a li-dl zing ich mir, zing ich mir.
And a song I'm sing-ing, I'm sing-ing clear.

| Am | E7 | Am Dm Am B7 |

Tsu der shtot iz vayt noch, zeyer vayt,

Em | B7 | Em Am Em E7
Shteyt a kretshme bay der zayt, bay der zayt,

Am | Dm | Am E7 Am A7
Breyt tseefnt iz di tir, iz di tir.

Dm | E7 | Am Dm Am
Kretshmer, gib a glezl, a glezl mir!

Am | E7 | Am Dm Am B7
Noch a glezl, noch eyns, noch a gloz

Em | B7 | Em Am Em E7
Gist mir on der bale—der balebos.

Am | Dm | Am E7 Am A7
Vos mir shtot un ven mir, ven yarid,

Dm | E7 | Am Dm Am
Az keyn ferdl darf ich nit, darf ich nit.

Am | E7 | Am Dm Am B7
S'ferdl hob ich nit gekoyft, nit gekoyft,

Em | B7 | Em Am Em E7
Un dos gelt shoyn lang farzoyft, lang farzoyft,

Am | Dm | Am E7 Am A7
Un far tsores shpring ich mir, shpring ich mir,

Dm | E7 | Am Dm Am
Un a lidl zing ich mir, zing ich mir.

Am | E7 | Am Dm Am B7
But the town is far off, it's far away.

Em | B7 | Em Am Em E7
I come to a tavern along the way.

Am | Dm | Am E7 Am A7
And the door is open, it's open wide,

Dm | E7 | Am Dm Am
So to wet my whistle I step inside.

Am | E7 | Am Dm Am B7
I'll just have another and then one more.

Em | B7 | Em Am Em E7
Willingly a glassfull the boss does pour.

Am | Dm | Am E7 Am A7
Where was I just going with all this speed—

Dm | E7 | Am Dm Am
To buy a horse? That's something I do not need.

Am | E7 | Am Dm Am B7
I didn't buy the horse, that's all I can say.

Em | B7 | Em Am Em E7
And my money long since is drunk away.

Am | Dm | Am E7 Am A7
And my troubles make me keep springing on,

Dm | E7 | Am Dm Am
And a song I'm singing—I'm singing on.

74

DOS LIDL FUN BROYT
THE SONG OF BREAD

By **MARK WARSHAWSKY**

Groy - ser got! mir zing - gen li - der, Un - dzer hilf bis - tu a -
Might - y God! we're sing - ing to ___ you, For us you're the on - ly

leyn; Nemt tsu - noyf di sno - pes, bri - der, Biz di
one. Gath - er up the wheat-sheaves broth - ers, Till the

1.
zun vet un - ter - geyn. Nemt tsu -
set - ting of the sun. Gath - er

2.
zun vet un - ter - geyn.
set - ting of the sun.

C   Dm
Zol di zun undz brein, brotn,
G7   C
Zi hot undz geshaynt tsum glik;
F   C
Zet dos broyt iz undz gerotn,
G7   C
Kinder, keyn mol nit tsurik.   2

C   Dm
Zoln undzere kinder visn
G7   C
Fun a lebn oyf der velt,
F   C
Az dos broyt, un yeder bisn
G7   C
Iz fun undzer eygn feld.   2

C   Dm
Though the sun should bake or burn us,
G7   C
We have reaped joy from its rays.
F   C
With our bread no one can spurn us—
G7   C
Never back to the old days.   2

C   Dm
Let our children know the blessings
G7   C
Of a life upon the earth.
F   C
For the bread that we are eating
G7   C
From our fields has proved our worth.   2

75

A CHAZANDL OYF SHABES
A CANTOR FOR THE SABBATH

Slowly and freely, in cantorial style

Iz ge-ku-men tsu fo-rn a cha-zan in a kleyn shte-tl,
Once a can-tor ar-rived in a ti-ny lit-tle vil-lage, To

Da-ve-nen a sha-bes, Oy, da-ve-nen sha-bes.____
sing the Sab-bath ser-vice, To sing the Sab-bath ser-vice.____

Zay-nen ge-ku-men im her-rn di dray shen-ste ba-le-
And just to lis-ten to him sing the ser-vice came the three

ba-tim-fun dem shte-tl: ____ Ey-ner a shnay-der-l, der
big men of the vil-lage.____ One was a tai-lor, the

tzvey-ter a ko-val-tshik-l. un der drit-ter a ba-le-gol-tshik-l.
sec-ond was a black-smith, and the third was a wag-on driv-er.

Verses

Ruft zich o-pet der shnay-der-l, Ruft zich o-pet der shnay-der-l. "Oy!____
Then the tai-lor spoke up, Yes, the tai-lor spoke up and said, "Oh!____

____ hot er ____ ge-da-vnt, hot er ____ ge-da-vnt! A-
how he ____ did sing ____ it, how he ____ did sing ____ it! The

zoy vi men git ____ mit-n no-dl a shtoch, ____ Un mit-n
way that a nee-dle would give a quick stitch, ____ Or the hot

ey - sen, oy, a press. ____ Oy, ____ hot er ge - da - vnt.
i - ron a good press. ____ Oh, ____ how he did sing it,

Oy, oy, oy, ____ oy, ____ oy, ____ oy!
Oh, oh, oh, ____ oh, ____ oh, ____ oh!

Oy, hot er ____ ge - da - vnt!" ____
Oh, how he ____ did sing ____ it!" ____

D
Ruft zich opet dos kovaltshikl,

Ruft zich opet dos kovaltshikl,
       Am   D Am
"Oy! hot er gedavnt, hot er gedavnt!
 D
Azoy vi men git mitn hammer, oy, a zets,

Un mit di kletshes, oy, a kvetch,
B7   Em
Oy, hot er gedavnt!
A7 D Bm
Oy, oy, oy, oy, oy, oy!
A7sus4   A7 D
 Oy, hot er gedavnt!"

 D
Ruft zich opet dos balegoltshikl,

Ruft zich opet dos balegoltshikl,
       Am   D Am
"Oy, hot er gedavnt, hot er gedavnt!
 D
Azoy vi men git mit di laytses, oy, a tsi,

Un mitn baytshel, oy, a chvatsh.
B7   Em
Oy, hot er gedavnt!
A7 D Bm
Oy, oy, oy, oy, oy, oy!
A7sus4   A7 D
Oy, hot er gedavnt!"

 D
Then the blacksmith spoke up,

Yes, the blacksmith spoke up, and said,
       Am   D Am
"Oh, how he did sing it, how he did sing it!
 D
The way that a hammer would give a sharp blow,

Or the bellows a hard squeeze,
B7   Em
Oh, how he did sing it!
A7 D Bm
Oh, oh, oh, oh, oh, oh!
A7sus4   A7 D
Oh, how he did sing it!"

 D
Then the driver spoke up,

Yes, the driver spoke up, and said,
       Am   D Am
"Oh, how he did sing it, how he did sing it!
 D
The same way that a driver would pull on the reins,

Or crack his whip hard in the air,
B7   Em
Oh, how he did sing it!
A7 D Bm
Oh, oh, oh, oh, oh, oh!
A7sus4   A7 D
Oh, how he did sing it!"

BAYT ZHE MIR OYS A FINFUNTSVANTSIKER
CHANGE FOR ME THIS TWENTY-FIVER

Song of the wedding guest.

Bayt zhe mir oys a finf-un-tsvan-tsi-ker* Oyf sa-me-rod-ne
Change for me, please, this twen-ty-fiv-er In-to a brand-new

dray-er; Un shpilt zhe mir, klez-mo-rim-lech A li-de-le, a tay-er.
three-er. And play for me, mu-si-cians, play, The song that I hold dear.

Chorus

Yam-tshe-ram-tshi, yam-tshe-ram-tshi, Yam-tshe-ram-tshi, yam-tshe-ray; yam-tshe-ray!

Em	Am Em
Bay zhe mir oys a finfuntsvantsiker	
B7 Em	
Oyf samerodne firer;	
Am	
Un shpilt zhe mir, klezmorimlech,	
B7 Em	
Dos zelbike, vos frier. *Chorus*	

Em   Am Em
Change for me, please, this twenty-fiver
   B7   Em
Into a brand-new four,
              Am
And play for me, musicians, play,
   B7   Em
The one you played before. *Chorus*

Em   Am Em
Bayt zhe mir oys a finfuntsvantsiker,
   B7   Em
Oyf samerodne tsener;
              Am
Un shpilt zhe mir, klezmorimlech,
   B7   Em
Dos zelbike, nor shener. *Chorus*

Em   Am Em
Change for me, please, this twenty-fiver
   B7   Em
Into a brand-new ten,
              Am
And play for me, musicians, play,
   B7   Em
The same song once again. *Chorus*

Em   Am Em
Bayt zhe mir oys a finfuntsvantsiker
  B7   Em
Oyf same imperyaln;
              Am
Ich vel betn di klezmorimlech,
   B7   Em
Zey zoln zich nit ayln. *Chorus*

Em   Am Em
Change for me, please, this twenty-fiver,
   B7   Em
This gold coin's theirs, don't worry;
              Am
And I will ask all the musicians, please,
   B7   Em
To play but not to hurry. *Chorus*

*Ruble note, that is.

78

ALE MENTSHEN TANTZENDIK
FOLKS ARE THEIR DANCINGEST

Lively

A - le ment-shen tan - tzen - dik un shprin-gen - dik un lach - en - dik un
Folks are at their danc - ing - est and jump - ing - est and laugh - ing - est and

zin - gen - dik, Un Moy - she - le shteyt als vey - nen - dik. Moy - she, Moy - she,
sing - ing - est, But Moy - she - le just keeps cry - ing on. Moy - she, Moy - she,

vus, du veynst?_ Ich veyn,_ vus ich meyn,_ Es iz shoyn tzayt tzu der chu - pe tzu geyn.
why d'you cry?___ I cry,___ tell you why,___ It's time to go to the chu - pe*, oh my!

Each verse begins with a repeat of the first eleven measures of text.

    Em   B7 Em
. . . Es iz shoyn tsayt esn tsu geyn!

       Em   B7 Em
. . . It's time to start feasting, oh, my!

    Em   B7   Em
. . . Es iz shoyn tsayt a mitsve tentsl geyn!

     Em   B7   Em
. . . It's time to dance with the couple, oh, my!

     Em   B7   Em
. . . Es iz shoyn tsayt shlofn tsu geyn!

       Em   B7   Em
. . . It's time that we were all sleeping, oh, my!

*Chupe—the wedding canopy.

A GLEZELE LECHAYIM
A TOAST TO LIFE

By **BERGOTZ** and **PULVER**

A gle - ze - le le - cha - yim, es shat nit nem - n haynt, Ven men
A toast to life, let's raise up, let's drink it down to - day, As we

est ba a yon - tev - dik - n tish. _____ A gle - ze - le le -
feast on this hap - py hol - i - day. _____ A toast to life, let's

cha - yim, far fraynt-shaft un far fraynt, Men zol shten - dik nor mun - ter zayn, un
raise up for friend-ship and for friends, May we al - ways be live - ly and be

frish. _____ A gle - ze - le le - cha - yim, far alt un yung vos zits - n do, For
gay. _____ A toast to life, let's raise up for old and young who are now here, And

ye - der - n be - zun - der vos zay - nen haynt mit unz ni - to. A gle - ze - le le -
al - so for the oth - ers, though miss - ing, we hold ver - y dear. A toast to life, let's

cha - yim, dem bech - er ful mit vayn, Far der zun, zi zol shten - dik mit unz zayn. ___
raise up, so fill the glass with wine, For the sun, may it al - ways bright-ly shine. ___

```
Em                Am   B7  Em
A glezele lechayim, mayn tost vet zayn atsind,
      G                       E7
Nor af simches far yedern fun aych.
Am              Dm  E7  Am
A glezele lechayim far foter un far kind,
      C                  B7
Az mit freyd, di mame zol zayn raych.
     E7
A glezele lechayim, nit opshteyn zol fun
   Am
   unz di shayn,
      D7                      B7
Kayn shvartser tog in lebn in der mishpoche
   Em   B7
   zol nit zayn.

Em              Am   B7  Em
A glezele lechayim iz oystrinkn keday,
      G           Am  B7  Em
Ven men zet zich mit fraynt fun dos nay.


Em                Am  B7   Em
A glezele lechayim, far unzer groyser land,
   G                       E7
Iber unz zol der himl kukn reyn.
Am            Dm   E7      Am
A glezele lechayim, ich vintsh aych noch anand,
      C                   B7
Mit a shmechl oyf di lipn zolt ir geyn.
     E7
A glezele lechayim, bagleytn zol aych
   Am
   shtendik freyd,
      D7                     B7
Mit layblichn un munter, ir zolt keynmol
   Em    B7
   nit tsesheyd.

Em                 Am   B7  Em
A glezele lechayim, far alts vos unz gefelt,
      G        Am  B7   Em
Un far sholem oyf gor der gantser velt.
```

```
Em                  Am  B7   Em
A toast to life, let's raise up, it simply goes like this:
   G                       E7
Only joy do I wish to each of you!
Am                   Dm  E7  Am
A toast to life let's raise up, may nothing go amiss,
   C                          B7
For the parents and child their whole life through.
     E7
A toast to life, let's raise up, and may the sun shine
   Am
   merrily,
      D7                       B7
And may no days of darkness descend upon our
   Em  B7
   family.

Em                     Am   B7   Em
A toast to life, let's raise up, it's good to drink it down,
      G       Am       B7   Em
When we see our friends from all around.


Em                   Am   B7  Em
A toast to life, let's raise up, to our beloved land,
   G                       E7
May the heavens above hear our song.
Am                   Dm   E7   Am
A toast to life, let's raise up, I wish you once again,
   C                          B7
With a smile on your lips your whole life long.
     E7
A toast to life, let's raise up, may gladness cheer you
   Am
   every day,
      D7                         B7
Your nearest and your dearest shall never ever
   Em  B7
   go away.

Em                    Am    B7    Em
A toast to life, let's raise up, for all that we hold dear,
      G       Am      B7    Em
May the world live in peace, and without fear!
```

CHATSKELE, CHATSKELE

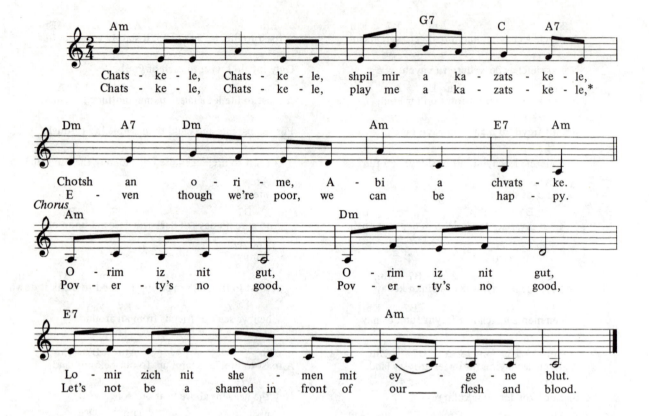

Chats - ke - le, Chats - ke - le, shpil mir a ka - zats - ke - le,
Chats - ke - le, Chats - ke - le, play me a ka - zats - ke - le,*

Chotsh an o - ri - me, A - bi a chvats - ke.
E - ven though we're poor, we can be hap - py.

Chorus

O - rim iz nit gut, O - rim iz nit gut,
Pov - er - ty's no good, Pov - er - ty's no good,

Lo - mir zich nit she - men mit ey - ge - ne blut.
Let's not be a shamed in front of our____ flesh and blood.

Am   G7 C A7
Nit kayn gebetene, aleyn gekumen,

 Dm A7 Dm Am E7 Am
Chotsh an orime, fort a mume. *Chorus*

Am   G7 C A7
Chatskele, chatskele, shpil mir a dume,

 Dm A7 Dm Am E7 Am
Chotsh an orime, abi a frume. *Chorus*

Am   G7 C A7
We're uninvited, we came anyway,

 Dm A7 Dm Am E7 Am
Even though she's poor, Auntie, please let her stay. *Chorus*

Am   G7 C A7
Chatskele, Chatskele, come on now and play for me,

 Dm A7 Dm Am E7 Am
Even though we're poor, still pious Jews are we. *Chorus*

Kazatskele—diminutive of *kazatske,* a fast Cossack dance.

HEY! ZHANKOYE

Zhankoye was a Jewish settlement in the Crimea in the 1930s. It was completely de[stroyed by the] Germans during the war.

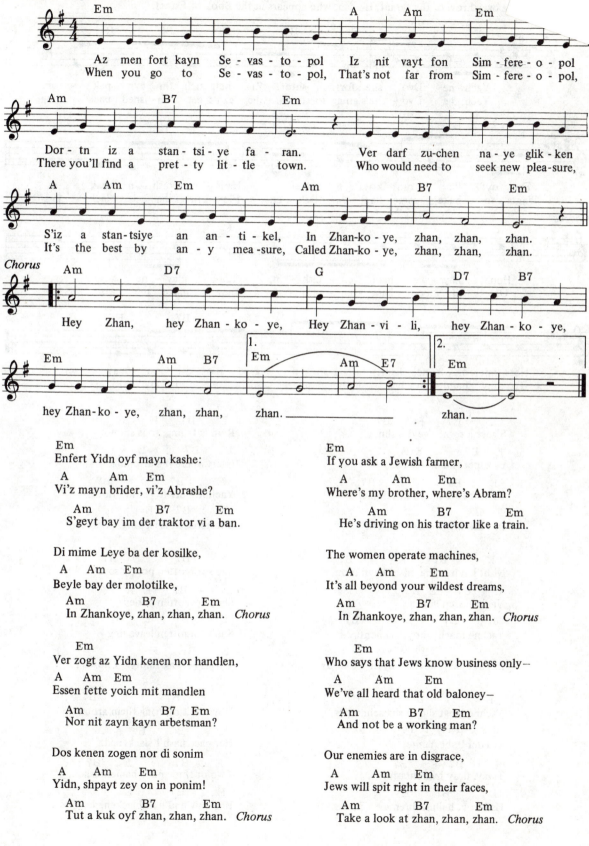

Em
Enfert Yidn oyf mayn kashe:

A   Am   Em
Vi'z mayn brider, vi'z Abrashe?

Am   B7   Em
S'geyt bay im der traktor vi a ban.

Di mime Leye ba der kosilke,

A   Am   Em
Beyle bay der molotilke,

Am   B7   Em
In Zhankoye, zhan, zhan, zhan. *Chorus*

Em
Ver zogt az Yidn kenen nor handlen,

A Am Em
Essen fette yoich mit mandlen

Am   B7 Em
Nor nit zayn kayn arbetsman?

Dos kenen zogen nor di sonim

A   Am   Em
Yidn, shpayt zey on in ponim!

Am   B7   Em
Tut a kuk oyf zhan, zhan, zhan. *Chorus*

Em
If you ask a Jewish farmer,

A   Am   Em
Where's my brother, where's Abram?

Am   B7   Em
He's driving on his tractor like a train.

The women operate machines,

A   Am   Em
It's all beyond your wildest dreams,

Am   B7   Em
In Zhankoye, zhan, zhan, zhan. *Chorus*

Em
Who says that Jews know business only—

A   Am   Em
We've all heard that old baloney—

Am   B7   Em
And not be a working man?

Our enemies are in disgrace,

A   Am   Em
Jews will spit right in their faces,

Am   B7   Em
Take a look at zhan, zhan, zhan. *Chorus*

83

HAMENTASHN

Hamentashn are traditional, triangular-shaped pastries baked during the holiday of Purim. They commemorate the overthrow of the tyrant, Haman, who appears in the Book of Esther.

Yach-ne Dvo-she fort in shtot, Zi halt zich in eyn-pak-n,
Yach-ne Dvo-she's going to town, She can't get fin-ished pack-ing,

Far oyf Pu-rim koyf-n mel, Ham-en-tash-n bak-n.
Wants to bake some ham-en-tash-en, Flo-ur she is lack-ing.

Chorus

Hop, may-ne ham-en-tash-n, hop, may-ne vay-se,
Oh, my poor ham-en-tash-n, they make me wor-ry,

Hot mit may-ne ham-en-tash-n grod pas-irt a may-se.
To my ham-en-tash-en hap-pened such a fun-ny sto-ry.

E B7 E B7 S'geyt a regn, s'geyt a shney	E B7 E B7 Rain is falling, so is snow,
E B7 E A Es kapet fun di decher.	E B7 E A Everywhere it's dripping.
E B7 E B7 Yachne fort shoyn koyfn mel	E B7 E B7 Yachne's off to get her flour,
E B7 E In a zak mit lecher. *Chorus*	E B7 E But her sack is ripping. *Chorus*
E B7 E B7 Nisht kayn honig, nisht kayn mon,	E B7 E B7 She's forgotten poppy seeds,
E B7 E A Un fargessen heyvn,	E B7 E A She's forgotten honey.
E B7 E B7 Yachne macht shoyn hamentashn,	E B7 E B7 She's forgotten leavening—
E B7 E Es bakt zich shoyn in oyvn. *Chorus*	E B7 E This is getting funny. *Chorus*
E B7 E B7 Yachne trogt shoyn shalachmones,	E B7 E B7 Now she's offering them around,
E B7 E A Tsu der bobe Yente,	E B7 E A Her pace hasn't slackened.
E B7 E B7 Tsvey, dray hamentashn	E B7 E B7 Two or three poor hamentashen,
E B7 E Halb-roy, halb-farbrente. *Chorus*	E B7 E Half-raw and half-blackened. *Chorus*

84

BIROBIDJAN

In 1934 a part of the far-eastern Khabarovsk oblast of the Soviet Union, near the Chinese border, was set aside as a Jewish region. It was called Birobidjan. Despite optimistic songs like this one, it never really attracted the mass of the prewar Russian Jewish population.

A' chay! A' chay! So - vyet - n macht hot land ge - geb - n,
To life! To life! The So - viets gave us fer - tile land, The

Boyt der yid a nay - em leb - n. Bi - ro, Bi - ro,__
Jew can build with his own hand.

Chorus

Bi - ro, Bi - ro,__ Bi - ro, Bi - ro,__ Bi - ro - bi - djan. Be - ro - bi - djan.

Dm
A' chay! A' chay!

Eygene milch un eygene korn,

Filt der yid vi nay geborn. *Chorus*

Dm
A' chay! A' chay!

Bleyen vegn vachsn gasn,

Oysgefortselt has fun rasn. *Chorus*

Dm
A' chay! A' chay!

M'nachem Mendels tantsn chvatske,

Mit Kosakn a kazatske. *Chorus*

Dm
To life! To life!

We have our milk and our corn,

The Jew feels just like a newborn. *Chorus*

Dm
To life! To life!

New streets spring up in empty places,

Brotherhood between all races. *Chorus*

Dm
To life! To life!

There's been a great change in the weather,

Jew and Cossack dance together. *Chorus*

VI AZOY TRINKT A KEYSER TEY?
HOW DOES A TSAR DRINK TEA?

Each verse begins with a repeat of the first ten measures of text.

Am B7 Em
Vi est a keyser bulbes?

Me shtelt avek a vant mit puter,

       Am
Un a soldatl mit a harmatl

Em
Shist durch di puter mit a heyser bulbe,

Un treft dem keyser glaych in moyl arayn.

     .C
Oy, ot azoy, oy ot azoy

Am B7 Em
Est a keyser bulbes.

Am B7   Em
How does a tsar eat potatoes?

You raise up a big wall of butter,

       Am
And a soldier with a cannon

Em
Shoots a hot potato through the butter,

And hits the tsar right in the mouth.

       C
And that's how, and that's how

Am   B7   Em
Tsars eat potatoes.

Am   B7   Em
Vi shluft a keyser bay nacht?

Me shitt un a fuln cheyder mit feydern,

                    Am
Un me shlaydert arayn ahintsu dem keyser,

  Em
Un dray rotes soldatn shteyen un shrayen:

"Sha! Sha! SHA!"

Oy, ot azoy, oy, ot azoy,

Am   B7   Em
Shluft a keyser bay nacht!

Am   B7   Em
How does a tsar sleep at night?

You fill up a room with feathers,

              Am
And you throw the tsar into it.

      Em
And three companies of soldiers stand and shout,

"Sha! Sha! SHA!"

And that's how, and that's how

Am   B7   Em
Tsars, they sleep at night.

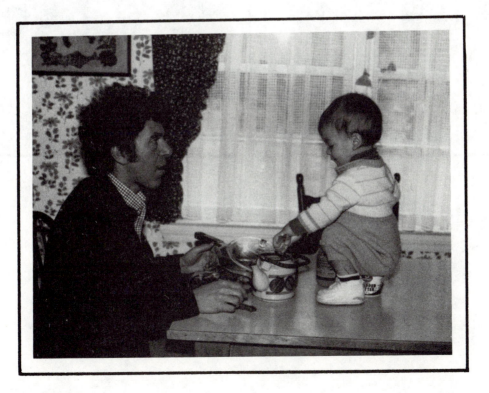

ACHTSIK ER UN ZIBETSIK ZI
EIGHTY HE AND SEVENTY SHE

Es iz hay-nt a-ku-rat ge-vo-rn fuf-tsik yor, az zey
Well, to-day we mark the fif-tieth an-ni-ver-sa-ry, The old

le-bn shoyn in ey-nem dos al-te por. Zey ho-bn zich ge-el-tert,
cou-ple is to-geth-er so hap-pi-ly. They have both got-ten old-er,

kikt aych tsi, Ach-tsik er, un zi-be-tsik zi.
just you see, Eight-y he and sev-en-ty she.

Chotsh der zeyde mit der bobn zaynen
kurts un kleyn,
Nor der zayde mit der bobn zaynen mole
cheyn.
Er mitn shpitsichdikn berdele,
Achtsik er un zibetsik zi.

Though the grandpa and the grandma, they are
short and small,
Still the grandpa and the grandma are the best
of all.
He with his little pointed beard, just you see,
Eighty he and seventy she.

Zey zaynen haynt gegangen beyde in shul,
Un hobn dort gedavnt take ful.
Got hot zey geholfn, borochi,
Achtsik er un zibetsik zi.

Well, today they went together to the *shul,**
And both together they prayed their full.
God has helped them, don't you see?
Eighty he and seventy she.

Der oylem hot zich keyn aynhore gezetst
tsum tish,
Un az men hot aroyfgegebn di fayerdike
fish,
Hot a droshe gezogt Reb Hershele Tsvi:
Achtsik er un zibitsik zi.

When the guests, thank God, were seated and began
to eat,
The spicy fish was served up—what a
treat!
A toast was made by Reb Hershele Tsvee:
Eighty he and seventy she.

Shul—prayer house, synagogue.

DI MEZINKE OYSGEGEBN
MY YOUNGEST DAUGHTER'S MARRIED

Shtar - ker, be - ser! Di rod, di rod macht gre - ser!
Bet - ter, strong - er! Let's dance a lit - tle long - er!

Groys hot mich Got _____ ge-macht. Glik ___ hot er mir ___ ge-bracht.
God has ex - alt - ed me, He___ has made me ___ hap - py.

Hu - lyet kin - der a gan - tse nacht! Di me -
Let the par - ty just be _____ care - free! For my

zin - ke oys - ge - ge - bn! Di me - zin - ke oys - ge - ge - bn!
young - est daugh - ter's mar - ried! For my young - est daugh - ter's mar - ried!

Em	Em
Motl! Shimen!	Motl! Shimen!
E7 Am	E7 Am
Di orime layt zenen gekumen,	Here come poor men and women.
B7	B7
Shtelt zey dem shenstn tish,	Let them have a place to sit,
Em	Em
Tayere vaynen, tayere fish,	The wine, the fish—tasty bit.
Am B7	Am B7
Oy vey, tochter, gib mir a kish! *Chorus*	Kiss me, my child—imagine it! *Chorus*
Em	Em
Ayzik! Mazik!	Isaac! Be quick!
E7 Am	E7 Am
Di bobe geyt a kazik.	See grandma dance a *kazik.**
B7	B7
Keyn aynhore zet nor zet,	Lord protect her, just you see
Em	Em
Vi zi topet, vi zi geyt,	How she's stamping happily.
Am B7	Am B7
Oy, a simche, oy, a freyd. *Chorus*	What a party—can it be? *Chorus*

Kazik—a fast, lively Russian dance.

90

Em
Itsik! Shpitsik!

     E7   Am
Vos shvaygstu mit dem shmitsik?

        B7
Oyf di klezmer tu a geshrey:

    Em
Tsi shpiln zey, tsi shlofn zey?

  Am   B7
Rayst di strunes ale oyf tsvey! *Chorus*

Em
Izzy! Dizzy!

     E7   Am
Your fiddle should be busy!

        B7
To the bandsmen give a shout,

    Em
What's this silence all about?

  Am   B7
Make those strings sing or get out! *Chorus*

CH'BIN A BOCHER, A HULTAY
I'M A WANDERING FELLOW

Lively

Ch'bin a bo-cher, a hul-tay, Hob ich mir a shtek - n.
I'm a wan-der-ing fel-low, Some-thing of a rov - er.

Tri - li li-li, tri-li li-li-lay, Ch'shpan in al di ek - n.
Tri - li li-li, tri-li li-li-lay, And I've been all o - ver.

Dm Gm Dm Kum ich tsu a kretshme tsu	Dm Gm Dm I come to a friendly inn,
Gm Dm Klap ich on in toyer.	Gm Dm And I bang the knocker.
Gm Dm "Ver biztu? Ver biztu?"	Gm Dm "Who are you, say, who are you?"
A7 Dm Enfer ich: "A geyer."	A7 Dm I reply: "A walker!"
Dm Gm Dm "Leydig-geyer azoy fri,	Dm Gm Dm "Why so early, please tell us?
Gm Dm Chutspenik farshayter!"	Gm Dm Lazy good-for-nothing!"
Gm Dm Tri-li li-li, tri-li li-li-li,	Gm Dm Tri-li li-li, tri-li li-li-li,
A7 Dm Un ich gey mir vayter.	A7 Dm I continue wandering.
Dm Gm Dm Kum ich tsu a brunim tsu	Dm Gm Dm If I come upon a well,
Gm Dm Trink zich on mit vasser,	Gm Dm There my thirst I'm slaking.
Gm Dm Shtey ich in dem morgn groy	Gm Dm Like a wet hen I arise,
A7 Dm Vi a hon a nasser.	A7 Dm When the day is breaking.
Dm Gm Dm Fort a poyerl farbay:	Dm Gm Dm Comes a peasant riding by:
Gm Dm "Tso slichatsh na svetshe?"	Gm Dm "What's the latest news?"
Gm Dm Veys ich nit un tu a bray:	Gm Dm How should I know? And I shout,
A7 Dm "Svetshe, petshe, metshe!"	A7 Dm "Newsy—shmoozey—boozey!"

KUM AHER, DU FILOZOF
COME TO ME, PHILOSOPHER

Kum a - her, du fi - lo - zof, Mit dayn kor - tsn may - chl, __ Un
Come to me, phi - los - o - pher, And do not be fright - ened, __ And

zets zich tsu tsum re - bns tish, Dort ve - stu ler - nen sey - chl. __ Yam,
sit down at the rab - bi's desk, There you will be en - light - ened. __ Yam,

bam, bam, bam. Yam, bam, bam, bam. Yam, bam, bam, bam, bam, bam, bam. __ Yam,

bam, bam, bam. Yam, bam, bam, bam. Yam, bam, bam, bam, bam, bam, bam. __

Am Em	Am Em
A damf-shif hostu oysgeklert,	You designed a big steamboat,
D7 **G**	**D7** **G**
Un nemst zich mit dem iber;	It caused a big commotion,
Am **Em**	**Am** **Em**
Der rebe shpreyt zayn tichl oys	The rabbi spreads his handkerchief
Am **Em**	**Am** **Em**
Un shpant dem yam ariber. *Chorus*	And sails across the ocean. *Chorus*

Am Em	Am Em
A luft-balon hostu oysgetracht	You designed an air balloon,
D7 **G**	**D7** **G**
Un meynst du bist a chorets;	And you brag about it.
Am **Em**	**Am** **Em**
Der rebe shpot, der rebe lacht—	The rabbi scoffs—the rabbi laughs,
Am **Em**	**Am** **Em**
Er darf dos oyf kapores. *Chorus*	For he can fly without it. *Chorus*

Am Em	Am Em
Tsu veystu vos der rebe tit	What does our rabbi do
D7 **G**	**D7** **G**
Beshas er zitst bi'ychides—	When we alone do leave him?
Am **Em**	**Am** **Em**
In eyn minut er in himl flit	Up to the skies he quickly flies—
Am **Em**	**Am** **Em**
Un pravet dort shalesh-sides. *Chorus*	The heavenly hosts receive him. *Chorus*

Warsaw railroad station, 1938 *(Courtesy Dr. Irving Levitas)*

DI BAN
THE TRAIN

Tsu hot men a-zoyns ge - zen, tsu hot men a-zoyns ge - hert? Az
Did you ev - er see or hear a thing that had such a force? That

fa - yer un va - ser zol shle - pn vi a ferd? Oy,
fi - re and wa - ter could pull just like a horse? It

oy, hot er a fay - fer, Mit an ey - zer-nen koy - ech. Fun
has a pierc - ing whis - tle, Strength, it is so sur - pris - ing. The

un - ten gist zich va - ser, Fun oy - ven geyt a roy - ech.
wa - ter pours from un - der, A - bove the steam is ris - ing.

E   Am   E
Heyse koyln zenen far im a maychl,
    Am   E
Zudendik vaser zapt er in zayn baychl. *Chorus*

E   Am   E
Reboyne-shel-oylem, farkorts im zayne yoren,
    Am
Az Yidn apikorsim zoln nit kenen shabes
    E
forn. *Chorus*

E   Am   E
It delights in eating hot coals a-burning,
        Am   E
And the boiling water in its belly churning. *Chorus*

E   Am   E
Oh, dearest Lord God, preserve us from the devil,
                    Am
And do not let unpious Jews upon the Sabbath
        E
travel. *Chorus*

SHA! SHTIL!
SHH! QUIET!

Sha! Shtil! Macht nisht keyn ge-ri-der! Der re-be geyt shoyn
Sha! Shtil! Do not make a sound! For the rab-bi will soon

tan-tsn vi-der. Sha! Shtil! Macht nisht keyn ge-valt! Der re-be geyt shoyn
dance a-round. Sha! Shtil! Do not break his trance, The rab-bi is a-

tan-tsn bald. Un az der re-be tanst, Tan-tsn doch di vent;
bout to dance. And when he starts to dance, All the walls dance, too.

Lo-mir a-le-plyes-kn mit di hent.
Let us all now clap our hands, "one-two."

Dm
II Un az der rebe tantst,

Am
Tantst doch mit der tish,

F   Dm
Lomir ale topen mit di fis.

E
I Sha! Shtil! Macht nisht keyn gerider,

Am   E
Der rebe geyt shoyn zingn vider.

Sha! Shtil! Macht nisht keyn gevalt,

Am   E
Der rebe geyt shoyn tantsn bald.

Dm
II And when he starts to dance,

Am
Tables join the beat.

F   Dm
Let us all start stamping with our feet.

E
I Sha! Shtil! Talking would be wrong,

Am   E
The rabbi wants to sing a song.

Sha! Shtil! Do not say a thing,

Am   E
The rabbi is about to sing.

	Dm		Dm
II	Un az der rebe zingt	*II*	And when the rabbi sings

   Am
Dem heylign nign,

   Am
The holy melody,

F   Dm
Blaybt der sotn a toyter lign.

F   Dm
Satan falls for all eternity.

   E
I Sha! Shtil! Macht nisht keyn gerider,

   E
I Sha! Shtil! Talking would be wrong,

   Am   E
Der rebe geyt shoyn zingn vider.

   Am   E
The rabbi wants to sing a song.

Sha! Shtil! Macht nisht keyn gevalt,

Sha! Shtil! Do not say a thing,

   Am   E
Der rebe geyt shoyn zingn bald.

   Am   E
The rabbi is about to sing.

TSHIRIBIM

The chorus is a wordless Chassidic *nigun* (melody), to be sung and danced to with great joy.

LECHAYIM!
TO LIFE!

Gaily

Le - chay - im yi - de - lech! Le - chay - im bri - der - lech!
To life, my fel - low Jews! To life, my broth - er Jews!

Zingt zhe, trinkt zhe, A - le in a gu - ter sho!
Sing now, drink now, That is what good times are for!

To, lo - mir hul - ye - nen, A - rayn zich kul - ye - nen
Let's keep on swag - ger - ing, And we'll be stag - ger - ing

In dem gan - ey - dn, Bol - she ni - tshe - vo!
To Pa - ra - dise, And there is noth - ing more!

DER REBE ELIMELECH
RABBI ELIMELECH

Slow, free, ad lib

Em   B7

Az der Re - be E - li - me - lech Iz ge - vo - ren ze - yer frey - lach Iz ge -
E - li - me - lech, o - ur rab - bi, Once was feel - ing ver - y hap - py; El - i -

Em   C   G

vo - ren ze - yer frey - lach, E - li - me - lech,   Hot er
me - lech, He was feel - ing ver - y hap - py.   His phy -

E7   Am   B7   Em

oys - ge - ton di tfi - len Un hot on - ge - ton di bri - len Un hot ge -
lac - ter - ies he took off, And his glass - es near - ly shook off, And then he

Faster, in tempo   *Gradually faster until the end*

F#7   B7   Em

shikt noch di fi - dlers di tsvey.   Un az di fi - del - di - ke fi - dlers ho - bn
called for his fid - dlers to play.   And when the fid - dle play - ing fid - dlers start - ed

B7   Em   D7

fi - del - dik ge - fi - delt, Ho - bn fi - del - dik ge - fi - delt ho - bn
fid - dl - ing their fid - dles, Start - ed fid - dl - ing their fid - dles right a -

G   E7   Am

zey.   Un az di fi - del - di - ke fi - dlers ho - bn
way,   And when the fid - dle - play - ing fid - dlers start - ed

B7   Em   F#7   B7   Em

fi - del - dik ge - fi - delt Ho - bn fi - del - dik ge - fi - delt ho - bn zey.
fid - dl - ing their fid - dles, How those lit - tle fid - dle play - ers, they could play!

(continued)

101

Em
Un az der Rebe Elimelech

B7
Iz gevoren noch mer freylach,

Em   C   G
Iz gevoren noch mer freylach, Elimelech,

E7   Am
Hot er oysgeton dem hitl,

B7   Em
Un hot ongeton dem kitl,

F#7   B7   Em
Un hot geshikt noch di tsimblers, di tsvey.

Em
Un az di tsimbeldike tsimblers

B7
Hobn tsimbeldik getsimbelt,

Em   D7   G
Hobn tsimbeldik getsimbelt, hobn zey,

E7   Am
Un az di tsimbeldike tsimblers

B7   Em
Hobn tsimbeldik getsimbelt,

F#7   B7   Em
Hobn tsimbeldik getsimbelt, hobn zey.

Em
Un az der Rebe Elimelech

B7
Iz gevoren gor gor freylach,

Em   C   G
Iz gevoren gor gor freylach, Elimelech,

E7   Am
Hot er zich gemacht havdole,

B7   Em
Un geshikt rifn dem shames Naftole,

F#7   B7   Em
Un hot geshikt noch di payklers, di tsvey.

Em
Un az di paykeldike payklers

B7
Hobn paykeldik gepaykelt,

Em   D7   G
Hobn paykeldik gepaykelt, hobn zey,

E7   Am
Un az di paykeldike payklers

B7   Em
Hobn paykeldik gepaykelt,

F#7   B7   Em
Hobn paykeldik gepaykelt, hobn zey.

Em
Elimelech, our rabbi,

B7
Started feeling still more happy,

Em   C   G
Elimelech started feeling still more happy.

E7   Am
Then his cap, it went a-twirling,

B7   Em
And his cape, it went a-swirling,

F#7   B7   Em
And his tsimbalom players did play.

Em
And when the tsimbaloming tsimblers

B7
Started tsimble-tsimble-tsimbling,

Em   D7   G
Started tsimble-tsimble-tsimbling, right away,

E7   Am
And when the tsimbaloming tsimblers

B7   Em
Started tsimble-tsimble-tsimbling,

F#7   B7   Em
How those nimble tsimbalomers, they could play!

Em
Elimelech, our rabbi,

B7
He was feeling oh so happy,

Em   C   G
Elimelech, he was feeling oh so happy,

E7   Am
So he said the prayer *Havdole*,*

B7   Em
And he called for Reb Naftole,

F#7   B7   Em
And he called for his drummers to play.

Em
And when the drummers started drumming,

B7
On their drums they were rum-tumming,

Em   D7   G
On their drums they were rum-tumming, right away.

E7   Am
And when the drummers started drumming,

B7   Em
On their drums they were rum-tumming,

F#7   B7   Em
Cool as cucumbers, those drummers, they did play!

Havdole—Sabbath prayer.

By this time Rabbi Elimelech is so
transported with joy that everything
gets hopelessly mixed up in a wildly
repeated last fast section.

    Em
Un az di fideldike tsimblers

    B7
Hobn paykeldik gefidelt,

    Em   D7 G
Hobn paykeldik gefidelt, hobn zey,

      E7   Am
Un az di tsimbeldike payklers

    B7   Em
Hobn fideldik getsimbelt,

    F♯7   B7   Em
Hobn paykeldik gefidelt, hobn zey.

         Em
And when the fiddlers started drumming

       B7
On their tsimbaloms, so cunning,

       Em   D7 G
On their drimble-tsimble-fiddles, right away,

          E7   Am
And when the rum-tum-tumming drummers

      B7   Em
Fiddled with the tsimbalomers,

      F♯7   B7   Em
How those tsimble-fiddle-ummers, they could play!

It's Hard To Be A Jew

Warsaw, 1938 *(Courtesy Dr. Irving Levitas)*

MOYSHELE, MAYN FRAYND
MOYSHELE, MY FRIEND

See note on page 184.

By **MORDECHAI GEBIRTIG**
(1877-1942)

Vos mach-stu epes, Moy-she-le? Ch'der-ken dich noch on blik, Du
So how're you do-ing, Moy-she-le? You have-n't changed you know. You

bist ge-ven mayn cha-ve-rl Mit yo-rn fil tsu-rik, Un
used to be a pal of mine So man-y years a-go. We

oych in chey-der ho-bn mir Ge-le-rnt lang ba-nand, Ot
went to Che-der* side by side, We were a hap-py band. I

shteyt far mir der re-be noch, Der kan-tshik in zayn hant.
see the rab-bi e-ven now, The whip is in his hand.

Chorus

Oy, vu nemt men tsu-rik di yo-rn, Ye-ne shey-ne tsayt?
If we could but re-turn to those years, all those hap-py days.

Oy, dos yun-ge shey-ne le-bn Iz fun undz shoyn vayt.
All those good old days of child-hood now are far a-way.

Oy, vu nemt men tsu-rik di yo-rn, Moy-she-le, mayn fraynd?
If we could but re-turn to those years, Moy-she-le, my friend.

Oy, noch ye-nem bey-zn re-bn Benkt dos harts noch haynt.
E-ven for that mean old rab-bi I long with-out end.

After third verse:

Oy, noch ye-nem yun-ge lay-dn
E-ven for our youth-ful sor-rows

*Cheder—Hebrew school.

Am   A7
Vi geyt es epes Berelen,

Dm E7   Am
Avremele vos macht?

Dm
Un Zalmele un Yosele?

              Am
Zeyer oft fun aych getracht,

G7   C
Gecholemt fun aych, kinderlech,

G7   C
Gezen zich in der mit,

E7   Am
Gevorn alte yidelech—

F   E7
Vi shnel dos lebn flit. *Chorus*

Am   A7
Vos macht dayn shvester, Rochele?

Dm   E7   Am
Vi ich volt ir itst geseyn.

Dm
Zi iz amol, gedenkst du noch?

           Am
Tsum hartsn mir geveyn.

G7   C
Gelibt hot zi nor Berelen,

G7   C
Gehast mich on shum grund.

E7   Am
Farblibn iz in hartsn noch

F   E7
A nit kayn farheylte vund. *Chorus*

Am   A7
And how's it going with Berele?

Dm E7   Am
Avremele, him too?

Dm
And Zalmele and Yosele?

           Am
I've often thought of you.

G7   C
I've dreamed about you, all of you,

G7   C
You live in my mind's eye.

E7   Am
Now each of us is an old Jew—

F   E7
How swiftly life does fly. *Chorus*

Am   A7
How is your sister, Rochele?

Dm   E7 Am
Now, her I'd like to see.

Dm
She was one time, remember it?

          Am
So very dear to me.

G7   C
But she loved only Berele,

G7   C
For me had only scorn.

E7   Am
Yet to this day my heart remains

F   E7
Still wounded and forlorn. *Chorus*

TSUM HEMERL
TO THE HAMMER

Words by **ABRAHAM REISEN** (1875-1953)
Music by **A. M. BERNSTEIN** (1865-1932)

O, he-me-rl, he-me-rl, klap!— Shlog shtar-ker a tshvok noch a
O, ham-mer, o, ham-mer strike on!— The nails in the shoes that we

tshvok.— Keyn broyt iz in shtub shoyn ni-to,— Nor
mend.— There is not a crust of bread here,— Just

tso-res un leyd on an ek.— Keyn broyt iz in shtub shoyn ni-
sor-row and pain with-out end.— There is not a crust of bread

to,— Nor tso-res un leyd on an ek.
here,— Just sor-row and pain with-out end.

Dm	A	Dm

O, hemerl, hemerl, klap!

          A
Der zeyger, er shlogt shoyn bald tsvelf!

Dm   Gm   Dm
Di oygn zey machn zich tsu—

Gm   Dm   A
Gib koyech, o gotenyu, helf!

D7   Gm   Dm
Di oygn zey machn zich tsu—

Gm   A7   Dm
Gib koyech, o gotenyu, helf!

Dm   A   Dm
O, hammer, o, hammer, strike on!

          A
The clock will be soon striking twelve!

Dm   Gm   Dm
My eyes, they are closing with sleep—

Gm   Dm   A
Give strength to me, dear God, please help!

D7   Gm   Dm
My eyes, they are closing with sleep—

Gm   A7   Dm
Give strength to me, dear God, please help!

```
      Dm      A      Dm                        Dm        A        Dm
O, hemerl, hemerl, klap!                O, hammer, o, hammer, strike on!

                          A                                        A
Shlog shtarker di tshvekes, shlog gich!  Go faster, there's no time to lose.
   Dm        Gm        Dm                  Dm        Gm        Dm
Biz morgn muz fartik shoyn zayn          By morning the rich lady's girl
   Gm      Dm        A                      Gm        Dm        A
Der gviretes techterls shich.            Must have her brand-new pair of shoes.
   D7        Gm        Dm                   D7        Gm        Dm
Biz morgn muz fartik shoyn zayn          By morning the rich lady's girl
   Gm      A7      Dm                       Gm            A7        Dm
Der gviretes techterls shich.            Must have her brand-new pair of shoes.


   Dm      A      Dm                        Dm        A        Dm
O, hemerl, hemerl, klap!                O, hammer, o, hammer, strike on!

                          A                                        A
Nit glitsh fun mayn hant zich aroys!     We always are joined, you and I.
   Dm        Gm        Dm                  Dm        Gm        Dm
Mayn eyntsiker shpayzer bistu,           My only provider are you,
   Gm      Dm        A                      Gm        Dm        A
Fun hunger on dir gey ich oys!           Without you from hunger I'd die.
   D7        Gm        Dm                   D7        Gm        Dm
Mayn eyntsiker shpayzer bistu,           My only provider are you,
   Gm      A7      Dm                       Gm        A7        Dm
Fun hunger on dir gey ich oys.           Without you from hunger I'd die.
```

LOMIR ALE ZINGEN A ZEMERL
EVERYBODY SING A LITTLE SONG

The son asks the father the meaning of four Hebrew words: *lechem* (bread), *bosor* (meat), *dogim* (fish), and *matamim* (dessert). The father answers—in his own fashion, naturally . . . how else?

Lo - mir a - le zin - gen, lo - mir a - le zin - gen A
Ev - 'ry - bod - y sing now, ev - 'ry - bod - y sing now, a

ze - me - rl, a ze - me - rl: Le - chem iz broyt, —
lit - tle song, a lit - tle song: *Le - chem* is bread, —

Bo - sor ve - do - gim Ve - chol ma - ta - mim.
Meat and a fish and a lit - tle des - sert.

"Zog zhe mir ta - te - nyu, vos - iz le - chem?" "Bay di
"Tell me, then, fa - ther, dear, what — is *le - chem*?" "For the

groy - se ge - vi - rim iz le-chem a fri-shin-ke bul - ke-le, O-ber bay
rich and the might - y, oh, *le-chem*'s a fresh-ly baked lit - tle roll; Ah, but for

undz, kab - tso - nim, oy, dal - fo - nim, lz
us, poor peo - ple, oh, poor peo - ple, is

le - chem a da - re sko - rin - ke, ne - bech."
le - chem a dried — up crust of bread — too bad!"

110

     C
"Zog zhe mir, tatenyu, vos iz bosor?"

             G
"Bay di groyse negidim iz bosor a gebrotene

     C
     katshkele,

    G7   C   G7   C
Ober bay undz, kabtsonim, oy dalfonim,

                   F   C
Iz bosor a dare kishkele, nebech." *Chorus*

     C
"Zog zhe mir, tatenyu, vos is dogim?"

             G   C
"Bay di groyse negidim iz dogim a hechtele,

    G7   C   G7   C
Ober bay undz, kabtsonim, oy dalfonim,

                 F   C
Iz dogim an oysgeveykter hering, nebech." *Chorus*

     C
"Zog zhe mir, tatenyu, vos iz matamim?"

             G   C
"Bay di groyse negidim iz matamim kompot,

    G7   C   G7   C
Ober bay undz, kabtsonim, oy dalfonim,

                 F   C
Iz matamim gehakte tsores, nebech." *Chorus*

     C
"Tell me, o father dear, what is *bosor*?"

             G
"For the rich and the mighty, oh, *bosor*'s a roasted

     C
     duckling,

    G7   C   G7   C
But for us poor people, oh, poor people,

                         F   C
Bosor is a meager piece of derma*—too bad!" *Chorus*

     C
"Tell me, o father dear, what is *dogim*?"

             G   C
"For the rich and the mighty, oh, *dogim*'s a juicy pike,

    G7   C   G7   C
But for us poor people, oh, poor people,

                      F   C
Dogim is a tasteless piece of herring—too bad!" *Chorus*

     C
"Tell me, o father dear, what is *matamim*?"

             G   C
"For the rich and the mighty, oh, *matamim*'s compote,

    G7   C   G7   C
But for us poor people, oh, poor people,

                     F   C
Matamim is chopped-up troubles—too bad!" *Chorus*

---

*Derma—Beef or fowl casing stuffed with cereal and fat.

HIRSH LEKERT

On May 5, 1902, the shoemaker Hirsh Lekert attempted to assassinate the governor of Vilna, Von Vall. Lekert, a member of the Jewish Labor Bund, took this action in retaliation for the flogging of a group of workers who had taken part in a May Day demonstration. He was hanged on May 29, 1902.

By S. LEHMAN

In ballad style

A - zoy vi Hersh - ke iz fun shtub a - roys - ge -
As soon as Hersh - ke did go out of his a -

gan - gen, Ge - zogt hot er: a gu - tin - ke
part - ment, He wished us all a ver - y good

nacht. A - zoy vi Hersh - ke iz tsum tsirk tsu - ge -
night. As soon as Hersh - ke did ar - rive at the

gan - gen, A kley - ne vay - le hot er dort far - bracht.
cir - cus, He spent a while en - joy - ing the sight.

| | Am | Em | Am |
| Vi Hershke iz bay der lozhe geshtanen, |

Em Am
Zayn blik hot er gevorfn oyf vayt;

Dm G
Ven der gubernator iz fun tsirk aroysgegangen,

C G Am
Hot er im geshosn in a zayt.

Am Em Am
"Ay, brider, ir zolt zich nit dershrekn,

Em Am
Dem shtrik vos m'hot farvorfn oyf mir;

Dm G
Az mayn froy vet a zun geboyrn,

C G Am
A nomen zolt ir gebn noch mir.

Am Em Am
While Hershke was standing in the balcony,

Em Am
His glance wandered far and wide.

Dm G
When the governor walked out of the circus,

C G Am
He shot him in the side.

Am Em Am
"O brothers, please do not be frightened

Em Am
Of the rope they have thrown over me.

Dm G
When my wife will give birth to a son,

C G Am
You'll name him in my memory.

Am   Em   Am
"Ay, brider, ir zolt mich nit fargesn,

            Em   Am
Di velt vet mit mir noch ton klingen;

     Dm   G
Fun di tiranen nekome zolt ir nemen

   C   G   Am
Un a lid fun mir zolt ir zingen."

Am   Em   Am
"O brothers, please do not forget me,

           Em   Am
The world with my name will be ringing.

    Dm   G
Take vengeance on all of the tyrants,

    C   G   Am
And the song of my deeds keep on singing."

"Halt! Any weapons?" Picture postcard printed in Riga, Latvia, 1906.

DEM MILNERS TRERN
THE MILLER'S TEARS

This song refers to the expulsion of Jews from their villages—an all-too-common occurrence in Tsarist Russia.

By MARK WARSHAWSKY

Oy, vi - fl yo - rn Zay - nen far - fo - rn, Zayt
Could I but num - ber The years that slum - ber, Since

ich bin mil - ner ot o do? Di re - der drey - en zich, Di
I have been a mill - er here. The wheels keep turn - ing slow, The

yo - rn gey - en zich, Ich bin shoyn alt un grayz un gro. Di gro.____
years, they quick-ly go, And now I'm old and gray, I fear. The fear.____

G   D7
S'iz teg faranen,

G   D7
Ch'vil mich dermanen,

G   E7 Am
Tsi ch'hob gehat a shtikl glik?

D7
Di reder dreyen zich,

G
Di yorn geyen zich,

A7   D7   G E7
Keyn entfer iz nito tsurik.

Am   D7
Di reder dreyen zich,

G
Di yorn geyen zich,

A7   D7   G
Keyn entfer iz nito tsurik.

G   D7
Those days are gone by,

G   D7
And now I ask why:

G   E7   Am
Did happiness but smile on me?

D7
The wheels keep turning slow,

G
The years, they quickly go.

A7   D7   G E7
No answer ever do I see.

Am   D7
The wheels keep turning slow,

G
The years, they quickly go.

A7   D7   G
No answer ever do I see.

114

```
      G        D7
Ch'hob gehert zogn,

      G        D7
Me vil mich faryogn,

      G           E7   Am
Aroys fun dorf un fun der mil;

              D7
Di reder dreyen zich,

      G
Di yorn geyen zich,

      A7        D7  G  E7
Oy, on an ek un on a tsil.

      Am        D7
Di reder dreyen zich,

      G
Di yorn geyen zich,

      A7        D7  G
Oy, on an ek un on a tsil.


      G        D7
Vu vel ich voynen,

      G        D7
Ver vet mich shoynen?

      G           E7    Am
Ich bin shoyn alt, ich bin shoyn mid;

              D7
Di reder dreyen zich,

      G
Di yorn geyen zich,

      A7            D7     G  E7
Un oych mit zey geyt oys der yid.

      Am        D7
Di reder dreyen zich,

      G
Di yorn geyen zich,

      A7          D7    G
Un oych mit zey geyt oys der yid.
```

```
      G        D7
The order's given,

      G        D7
I will be driven

      G           E7   Am
All from my home and from the mill.

                    D7
The wheels keep turning slow,

      G
The years, they quickly go.

      A7               D7  G  E7
I have no place to live, and never will.

      Am            D7
The wheels keep turning slow,

      G
The years, they quickly go.

      A7               D7     G
I have no place to live, and never will.


      G        D7
Where can I go now?

      G        D7
I do not know now,

      G           E7  Am
For I am old and tired, too.

                    D7
The wheels keep turning slow,

      G
The years, they quickly go.

      A7           D7     G  E7
And with the years will go the Jew.

      Am            D7
The wheels keep turning slow,

      G
The years, they quickly go.

      A7           D7     G
And with the years will go the Jew.
```

Warsaw, 1938. *(Courtesy Dr. Irving Levitas)*

KESHENEVER POGROM
KISHINEV POGROM

The Kishinev pogrom took place in 1903. Forty-nine Jews were murdered and some five hundred injured. Jewish homes and property were destroyed. The pogrom was inspired by the age-old anti-Semitic legend, reborn every Passover/Easter, about the alleged Jewish need for the blood of a Christian child in religious services.

Dem er-shtn tog pey-sach Ho-bn
It was on Pass-o-ver's first day, that the

yi-de-lech gants frey-lech far-bracht. Un dem
Jew-ish peo-ple gath-ered in joy. And the

lets-tn tog cho-ge Hot men
last day of East-er, it was

Ke-she-nev cho-rev ge-macht.
Ki-she-nev that was de-stroyed.

E Am E Keshenev arumgeringlt	E Am E Kishinev was surrounded
E7 Am Azoy vi a bonder di fas,	E7 Am As a hoop holds a barrel's staves.
Dm Tates un mames un kinder	Dm Fathers and mothers and children
E Zaynen gefaln in gas.	E Right on the street found their graves.
E Am E Oy, du got in himl,	E Am E O, you God in heaven,
E7 Am Kuk shoyn arop tsu undz,	E7 Am Gaze downward if you choose,
Dm Batracht nor dem rash mit dem tuml,	Dm And look at the scene of destruction—
E Vi di goyim zenen zich noykem in undz.	E What the Gentiles are doing to Jews.

117

FONYE GANEV
FONYE, THE THIEF

"Fonye Ganev" ("Fonye the Thief") was the derisive code name for the tsar among Russian Jews. Conscription into "Fonye's Army" for periods of up to twenty-five years was a real and constant nightmare among Jewish boys aged twelve to eighteen. The following seven songs all deal with this subject.

With spirit

In droy - sn geyt a re - gn, Es vet doch zayn a blo - te,
Out - side the rain is fall - ing, The weath - er it is storm - y,

Haynt hot men mir op - ge - zogt Di per - ve le - go - te.
I was draft - ed just to - day In - to the tsar - ist ar - my.

Chorus

Fo - nye, fo - nye ga - nev, Fo - nye, fo - nye ga - nev,

Fo - nye, fo - nye ga - nev, fo - nye {blaybt a / is a} ga - nev.

Em	Em
Di mame hot mich gehodevet	My mama, she took care of me
Mit milch un mit puter,	With milk and with butter.
Am Em	Am Em
Itst darf ich fonyen dinen,	Now I have to serve the tsar—
B7 Em	B7 Em
Fintster iz mir un biter. *Chorus*	Oh, my lot is bitter. *Chorus*
Em	Em
Der rebe hot mich gelernt	The rabbi used to teach me
Chumesh mit rashe,	Pentateuch and Rashe.*
Am Em	Am Em
Itst darf ich fonyen dinen	Now I have to serve the tsar—
B7 Em	B7 Em
Far borshtsh un far kashe. *Chorus*	All for *borscht* and *kashe*.** *Chorus*

*The writings of Solomon ben Isaac (1040-1105), a French Hebrew scholar. He was also known as Rashi.
***Borscht*—vegetable soup, usually of beets. *Kashe*—buckwheat groats.

FONYE DINEN IZ ZEYER BITER
SERVING FONYE IS VERY BITTER

Em
Gantse necht shlof ich nish',

B7
Oyf mayne oygn kumt keyn shlof.

Am   A#dim
Dos hot doch mir keyn mentsh geton,

B7   Em
Dos iz doch nor fun got a shtrof.

Am   Em
Dos hot doch mir keyn mentsh geton,

B7   Em
Dos iz doch nor fun got a shtrof.

Em
Nights on end I lie awake,

B7
And I never close my eyes.

Am   A#dim
No man has done this thing to me,

B7   Em
But God has struck from the skies.

Am   Em
No man has done this thing to me,

B7   Em
But God has struck me from the skies.

FRAYTIK IN DER FRI
EARLY FRIDAY MORN

Fray-tik in der fri bakt men di cha-les, Oy, vey, ge-vald! Men
Ear-ly Fri-day morn *cha-les* are bak-ing, Oh, woe is me! And

nemt shoyn tsu di cha-sa-nim fun di ka-les, Oy, vey ge-vald! Men
from the brides all the bride-grooms they are tak-ing, Oh, woe is me! And

nemt shoyn tsu di cha-sa-nim fun di ka-les, Oy, vey ge-vald!
from the brides all the bride-grooms they are tak-ing, Oh, woe is me!

Em   E7
Fraytik tsu nacht macht men kidush,

   Am
Oy, vey, gevald!

             D7
Men kumt tsu loyfn oyf fonyes chidush,

   G
Oy, vey, gevald!

   Em   C
Men kumt tsu loyfn oyf fonyes chidush,

Em
Oy, vey, gevald!

Em   E7
Friday night we all make the blessing,

   Am
O, woe is me!

                 D7
The men in Fonye's uniform are dressing,

   G
O, woe is me!

   Em   C
The men in Fonye's uniform are dressing,

   Em
O, woe is me!

```
Em                    E7
Shabes in der fri est men fish,

    Am
    Oy, vey, gevald!

                              D7
Men nemt shoyn tsu di mener funem tish,

    G
    Oy, vey, gevald!

    Em                        C
Men nemt shoyn tsu di mener funem tish,

    Em
    Oy, vey, gevald!


Em                    E7
Shabes tsu nacht macht men havdole,

    Am
    Oy, vey, gevald!

                          D7
Men kumt tsu loyfn oyf fonyes mapole,

    G
    Oy, vey, gevald!

    Em                    C
Men kumt tsu loyfn oyf fonyes mapole,

    Em
    Oy, vey, gevald!
```

```
Em                        E7
Early on the Sabbath, fish is baking,

    Am
    O, woe is me!

                              D7
From the table our men they're taking,

    G
    O, woe is me!

Em                            C
From the table our men they're taking,

    Em
    O, woe is me!


Em                        E7
We say our prayers on Sabbath evening,

    Am
    O, woe is me!

                          D7
For the curséd army we are leaving,

    G
    O, woe is me!

    Em                    C
For the curséd army we are leaving,

    Em
    O, woe is me!
```

FARVOS ZOL ZAYN MAYN CHOSN A SOLDAT?
WHY SHOULD THEY MAKE A SOLDIER OF MY LOVE?

Kayn e - sn un kayn trin - kn, __ Ma - me, nemt mich nit. __ Ich
O moth - er, I've com - plete - ly __ lost my ap - pe - tite. __ As

gey a - rum __ shten - dig, shten - dig, vey - nen - dig. __ Ich freg nor bay dir,
I walk'round, my tears keep flow - ing day and night. __ I on - ly ask you,

tay - er - er Got: __ Far - vos zol zayn mayn cho - sn a sol - dat? __
dear __ God a - bove; __ Why should they make a sol - dier of my love? __

Am Dm E7 Am		Am Dm E7 Am
Ich vel zich tsushteln a leyterl,		I'll go and place a ladder up to heaven,
F B7 Em		F B7 Em
Un aroyfkrichn vel ich tsu Got.		And climb the rungs up to the Lord on high.
C G7 C Em		C G7 C Em
Ich vel bay im fregn eyne tsvey-dray verter:		And one-two-three I'll ask Him when I'm up above,
Am Dm E7 Am		Am Dm E7 Am
Far vos zol zayn mayn chosn a soldat?		Why should they make a soldier of my love?

Es volt zich oyfhoybn a shturim-vint,
I pray a storm will come and blow me far away,

Un avektrogn volt es mich tsu dir.
So I can be beside you once again.

Az ich zol derzen daynem sheynem kop hor,
And when your lovely hair once again I see,

Un take zich tsukushn oych mir dir.
I'll hold you and I'll kiss you tenderly.

Oy, du mayn tayerer Got!
Oh, tell me, God, how will I ever bear it?

Vi azoy vel ich dos kenen tsuzen?
I cannot look, the sight will just be too much.

Der keyser vet tsunmemen mayn tayern briliant,
The tsar will take my precious jewel from me,

Un vel ich darfn fun der vaytns shteyn.
And I'll be standing—watching helplessly.

Warsaw suburbs, 1938.   *(Courtesy Dr. Irving Levitas)*

ZAYZHE MIR GEZUNT
I MUST SAY FAREWELL

Mournfully

Zay - zhe mir ge - zunt, oy, zay - zhe mir ge - zunt, Mayn li - ber
I must say fare - well, oh, I must say fare - well, My dear - est

fu - ter! Ich for zich shoyn fun dir a - vek. Eyn - un - tzvan - tzik yor ____
fa - ther! I'm go - ing far a - way from you. Twen - ty one long years ____

hos - tu mich ge - ho - de - vit, Un itz - ter varf ich dich a - vek.
you have tak - en care of me, And now I must cast you a - side.

E   Am   E   Am
Zayzhe mir gezunt, oy, zayzhe mir gezunt

F   Dm   E
Mayne liber muter!

F   Dm   E
Ich for zich shoyn fun dir avek.

G7   C   F   E
Unter daynem hartsen hostu mich getrugen,

F   Dm   E
Un itster varf ich dich avek.

E   Am   E   Am
Zayzhe mir gezunt, oy, zayzhe mir gezunt,

F   Dm   E
Mayne getraye kale!

F   Dm   E
Ich for zich shoyn fun dir avek.

G7   C   F   E
Noch dir vel ich benkn besser vi noch ale,

F   Dm   E
Un itster varf ich dich avek.

E   Am   E   Am
I must say farewell, oh, I must say farewell,

F   Dm   E
My dearest mother!

F   Dm   E
I'm going away from you.

G7   C   F   E
Under your dear heart, oh mother, have you borne me,

F   Dm   E
And now I must cast you aside.

E   Am   E   Am
I must say farewell, oh, I must say farewell,

F   Dm   E
O my dearest bride!

F   Dm   E
I'm going away from you.

G7   C   F   E
More than for all others shall I long for you, dear,

F   Dm   E
And now I must cast you aside.

YOSHKE FORT AVEK
YOSHKE'S LEAVING NOW

Dating from the Russo-Japanese War of 1904–5, this moving song was intended to ridicule a certain unpleasant "Yoshke" from Vilna, who had been drafted. Over the years, however, the original intent has been lost and what remains is a tragic wartime dialogue.

Am

Koyf mir nit kayn lo - ke - nes un mach mich nit sheyn
Buy no pret - ty things for me, Don't make me look nice,

Dm6 — *E7*

Koyf dir a por - shti - ve - lech, Tsum pri - ziv darf - stu geyn.
But a pair of ar - my boots To march through snow and ice.

Chorus I
Dm6 — *E7*

Oy, —— oy, —— oy, —— oy, —— Yosh - ke fort a - vek.
Oh, —— oh, —— oh, —— oh, —— Yosh - ke's leav - ing now.

Dm6 — 3 — *E*

Noch a sho un noch a sho — Der po - yezd geyt a - vek.
In an - oth - er hour or so — The train is sure to go.

He: Am   Zay-zhe mir gezunt,

Mayn tayere kale.
Dm6
Noch dir vel ich benken
E7
Mer vi noch ale.

He: Am   Please take good care of yourself

My dearest bride,
Dm6
I will long for you,
E7
Till once again I'm by your side.

Chorus II
Dm6
Oy, oy, oy, oy,
E7
Yoshke fort avek.
Dm6
Noch a kush un noch a kush,
E
Der poyezd geyt avek.

Chorus II
Dm6
Oh, oh, oh, oh,
E7
Yoshke's leaving now.
Dm6
One more kiss, just one more kiss,
E
The train is sure to go.

126

Am
She: Di ban iz shoyn gekumen

Un es chapt mich on a shrek.
Dm6
Lomir zich gezegenen,

E7
Der poyezd geyt avek. *Chorus I*

Am
He: Klog-zhe nisht un veyn-zhe nisht

S'iz altsding blote!
Dm6
Ich vel zayn bay Fonyen

E7
Der shenster in der rote! *Chorus II*

Am
She: Droysn iz a zaveruche,

Droysn iz a shney,
Dm6
Oy vey, mamele,

E7
Dos kepele tut vey! *Chorus II*

Am
She: The train is in the station now,

It fills me with fear.
Dm6
We must say goodbye, my darling,

E7
Time is growing near. *Chorus I*

Am
He: Do not cry and do not weep,

It's not worth a cent.
Dm6
I will be the finest soldier

E7
In the regiment. *Chorus II*

Am
She: Outside there's a blizzard blowing,

And a deep snow.
Dm6
My God, Mother,

E7
How my head is filled with woe. *Chorus II*

DOS FERTSNTE YOR
IN NINETEEN-FOURTEEN

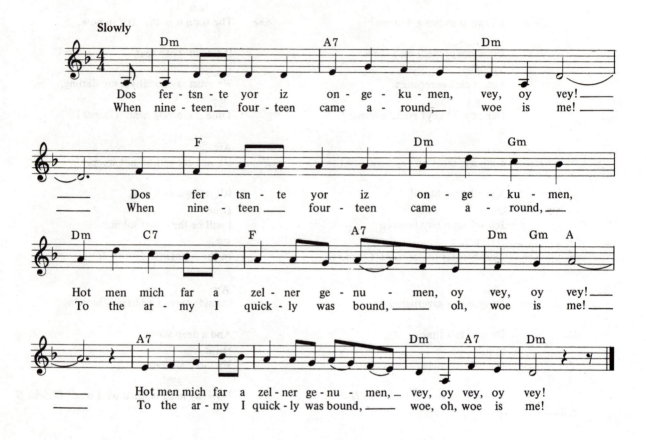

Dos fer - tsn - te yor iz on - ge - ku - men, vey, oy vey!____
When nine - teen___ four - teen came a - round,___ woe is me!____

____ Dos fer - tsn - te yor iz on - ge - ku - men,
____ When nine - teen___ four - teen came a - round,___

Hot men mich far a zel - ner ge - nu - men, oy vey, oy vey!____
To the ar - my I quick - ly was bound,___ oh, woe is me!____

____ Hot men mich far a zel - ner ge - nu - men, ___ vey, oy vey, oy vey!
____ To the ar - my I quick - ly was bound, ___ woe, oh, woe is me!

Dm   A7   Dm
Oyf di felder, grine felder, vey, oy vey!

F   Dm Gm
Oyf di felder, grine felder,

Dm C7 F   A7   Dm Gm A
Dortn ligt a gehargeter zelner, oy vey, oy vey!

A7   Dm A7 Dm
Dortn ligt a gerhargeter zelner, vey, oy vey, oy vey!

Dm   A7   Dm
On the green fields there is lying, woe is me!

F   Dm Gm
On the green fields there is lying

Dm C7 F   A7   Dm Gm A
Over there, a soldier dying, oh me, oh my!

A7   Dm A7 Dm
Over there, a soldier dying, woe, oh woe is me!

Dm   A7   Dm
Kumt a foygl on tsu flien, vey, oy vey!

  F   Dm   Gm
Kumt a foygl on tsu flien,

  Dm   C7   F   A7   Dm Gm A
Shtelt zich oyf mayn keyver ruen, oy vey, oy vey!

  A7   Dm   A7   Dm
Shtelt zich oyf mayn keyver ruen, vey, oy vey, oy vey!

  Dm   A7   Dm
Ver vet noch mich veynen un klogn, vey, oy vey!

  F   Dm   Gm
Ver vet noch mich veynen un klogn,

  Dm   C7   F   A7   Dm Gm A
Ver vet noch mir kadish zogn, oy vey, oy vey!

  A7   Dm   A7   Dm
Ver vet noch mir kadish zogn, vey, oy vey, oy vey!

  Dm   A7   Dm
Now a bird flies into sight, woe is me!

  F   Dm Gm
Now a bird flies into sight,

  Dm   C7   F   A7   Dm Gm A
On my grave it does alight, oh me, oh my!

  A7   Dm   A7   Dm
On my grave it does alight, woe, oh, woe is me!

  Dm   A7   Dm
Over me she'll mourn and cry, woe is me!

  F   Dm   Gm
Over me she'll mourn and cry,

  Dm   C7   F   A7   Dm Gm A
Who'll say Kaddish* when I die? Oh me, oh my!

  A7   Dm   A7   Dm
Who'll say Kaddish when I die? Woe, oh, woe is me!

*Kaddish—prayer for the dead.

A GANEYVE
A ROBBERY

Em   Am Em Am
Bay mayn rebin iz geveyzn,

Em Am Em   Am
Iz geveyzn bay mayn rebin,

Em   Am Em Am
Bay mayn rabin iz geveyzn

Em B7 Em
A ganeyve.

   G   D7 G
Ziben hemder vi di becher,

    D7 G
Dray mit lates, fir mit lecher.

Em   Am Em Am
Bay mayn rebin iz geveyzn

A#dim B7 Em
A ganeyve.

Em Am Em Am
At my rabbi's once it happened,

 Em Am   Em Am
Once it happened at my rabbi's,

Em Am Em Am
A disgraceful robbery,

 Em B7   Em
All at   my rabbi's.

    G   D7   G
Seven shirts the robber snatchéd,

           D7   G
Four were torn and three were patchéd.

Em Am Em Am
A disgraceful robbery,

 A#dim B7   Em
All at   my rabbi's.

Em   Am Em Am
Bay mayn rebin iz geveyzn,

Em Am Em   Am
Iz geveyzn bay mayn rebin,

Em   Am Em Am
Bay mayn rebin iz geveyzn

Em B7 Em
A   ganeyve.

     G   D7 G
    Ziben hayner vi di tsigl,

       D7   G
    Dray on kep un fir on fligl.

Em   Am Em Am
Bay mayn rebin iz geveyzn

A♯dim B7 Em
A   ganeyve.

Em   Am Em Am
Bay mayn rebin iz geveyzn,

Em Am Em   Am
Iz geveyzn bay mayn rebin,

Em   Am Em Am
Bay mayn rebin iz geveyzn

Em B7 Em
A   ganeyve.

    G   D7 G
    Ziben meyden vi di sosnes,

       D7   G
    Dray on tseyner—fir on yosnes.

Em   Am Em Am
Bay mayn rebin iz geveyzn

A♯dim B7 Em
A   ganeyve.

Em Am Em Am
At my rabbi's once it happened,

Em Am   Em Am
Once it happened at my rabbi's,

Em Am Em Am
A disgraceful robbery,

  Em B7   Em
All at   my rabbi's.

    G   D7   G
    Then the thief stole seven chickens,

        D7   G
    Headless, wingless--the plot thickens.

Em Am Em Am
 A disgraceful robbery,

  A♯dim B7   Em
All at   my rabbi's.

Em   Am Em Am
At my rabbi's once it happened,

  Em Am   Em   Am
Once it happened at my rabbi's,

Em Am Em Am
 A disgraceful robbery,

  Em B7 Em
All at   my rabbi's.

    G   D7   G
    Seven girls—the thief was ruthless,

        D7   G
    All were beauties—all were toothless.

Em Am Em Am
 A disgraceful robbery,

  A♯dim B7   Em
All at   my rabbi's.

HOT RACHMONES
HAVE COMPASSION

Yet another pogrom-inspired poem set to music (1909).

Words by **SIMEON S. FRUG** (1860-1916)
Music by **H. RUSSOTO**

Shtro - mn blut un tay - chn tre - rn, Zi - dn
Streams __ of blood and riv - ers of tears, __ Hot - ly

fli - sn tif __ un breyt. Und __ zer al - ter groy - ser
flow - ing deep __ and wide. For __ our old and ter - ri - ble

um - glik hot __ zayn hant __ oyf undz __ far - shpreyt. Hert __ ir
tor - ment is __ once more __ at __ our side. Lis - ten

dort vi mu - ters klo - gn, un __ fun kin - der dos __ ge -
there to moth - ers weep - ing, and __ to chil - dren's aw - ful

shrey. Toy - te li - gn in __ di ga - sn, kran - ke fa - ln ne - ben - zey.
shouts. Corp - ses ly - ing on __ the side - walks, sick ones fall - ing all - a - bout.

Bri - der, shves - ter, hot __ rach - mo - nes, Groys un shrek - lech iz di
Broth - ers, sis - ters, have __ com - pas - sion, Ter - ri - ble is o - ur

noyt. Git di toy - te oyf tak - ri - chim, Git di le - be - di - ke broyt.
need. Give the __ dead their de - cent __ shrouds, Give the liv - ing ones some bread.

MIT A NODL, ON A NODL
WITH A NEEDLE, OR WITHOUT ONE

Mit a no - dl, on a no - dl, Ney ich mir b'- ko - vod go - dol.
With a nee - dle, or with - out _ one, Sew - ing pleas - es this de - vout _ one.

Mit a no - dl, on a no - dl, Ney ich mir b'- ko - vod go - dol. Ich
With a nee - dle, or with - out _ one, Sew - ing pleas - es this de - vout _ one. I

ney un ney a gan - tze voch, _____ Ich ken shoyn ney - en a Par - iz - er loch. _
sew a week, it makes me smile, _____ I sew the lat - est Pa - ri - sian style. _

Mit a no - dl, on a no - dl, Ney ich mir b'- ko - vod go - dol.
With a nee - dle, or with - out _ one, Sew - ing pleas - es this de - vout _ one.

Am   Dm
Mit a nodl, on a nodl,

Em   Am
Ney ich mir b'kovod godl.

Dm
Mit a nodl, on a nodl,

Em   Am
Ney ich mir b'kovod godl.

  D   Dm
Ich tsi aroys di fastrige,

  Em   A
Un tu a lek fun mamelige.

Am   F
Mit a nodl, on a nodl,

Dm6   Am
Ney ich mir b'kovod godl.

Am   Dm
With a needle or without one,

Em   Am
Sewing pleases this devout one.

Dm
With a needle or without one,

Em   Am
Sewing pleases this devout one.

  D   Dm
And when I pull out all the basting,

  Em   A
It's time for *mamelige** tasting.

Am   F
With a needle or without one,

Dm6   Am
Sewing pleases this devout one.

*Mamelige—a Rumanian cereal or porridgelike delicacy made of cornmeal.

ZOL ICH ZAYN A ROV?
SHOULD I BE A RABBI?

Zol ich zayn a rov?___ Ken ich nit kayn Toy - re.
Should I be a rab - bi? Learn - ing, I've not an - y.

Zol ich zayn a soy - cher? Hob ich nit kayn schoy - re.
Should I be a mer - chant? I've not got a pen - ny.

Chorus

Un kayn hey___ hob ich nit. Un kayn hob - ber hob ich nit,
As for hay, ___ like - wise not. As for oats, ___ like - wise not.

Un a trunk bron - fn vilt___ zich, Un dos vibe ___ shilt ___ zich.
And a nice whis - key I could use, And my wife ___ does a - buse.

Zey ich mir a shteyn, Zetz ich mir un veyn. ___
On a stone near - by, I'll sit down and cry. ___

Em G
Zol ich zayn a shoychet?
Am Em
Halt ich nit keyn challef.
   G
Zol ich zayn a m'lamed?
Am Em
Ken ich nit keyn alef. *Chorus*

Em G
Should I be a butcher?*
Am Em
I don't have a cutter.
   G
Should I be a teacher?
   Am Em
My brain's just like butter. *Chorus*

Em G
Zol ich zayn a shuster?
 Am Em
Hob ich nit keyn kopete.
   G
Zol ich zayn a beker?
Am Em
Hob ich nit keyn lopete. *Chorus*

Em G
Should I be a cobbler?
Am Em
I'd live in a hovel.
   G
Should I be a baker?
Am Em
I don't have a shovel. *Chorus*

*The Yiddish word *shoychet* (Hebrew *shohet*) means the ritual slaugherer of animals in conformity with Jewish dietary laws (*kashrut*). There is no direct English equivalent.

134

Em   G
Zol ich zayn a koval?

     Am   Em
Hob ich nit keyn kovadle.

       G
Zol ich zayn a shenker?

Am   Em
Iz mayn vayb a pad'le. *Chorus*

Em   G
Should I be a blacksmith?

Am   Em
I don't have an anvil.

       G
Should I run a tavern?

    Am   Em
My wife drinks like the devil. *Chorus*

Кандидатъ въ раввины. No. 521. J. Kaufmann.   Rabbinatskandidat.
ערב רב

135

MAYKOMASHMALON
WHAT DOES IT MEAN?

A monologue of a Yeshiva student.

Thoughtfully

Am	Dm	Am	F

May - ko - mash - ma - lon der re - gen? Vos - zhe lust - er mir tzu
Does the rain have an - y mean - ing? Does it want to tell me

| Am | Dm | Am | F |

he - ren? Zay - ne trup - ens oyf di shoy - ben Kayke - len zich vi tri - be
some - thing? Lit - tle drops a - gainst the win - dows, Roll - ing down like some - one

| Am | Dm | Am | F |

tray - ren. Un di shti - vel iz tzu - ri - sen, Un es vert in gas a
cry - ing. And my boots are get - ting worn out, And the streets are wet and

| Am | Dm | Am | F |

blo - te; Bald vet oych der vin - ter ku - men, Ch'ob kayn va - re - me ka -
mud - dy; I don't have a win - ter great - coat, That can warm me as I

| Am | F | Em | A7 | C |

po - te. May - ko - mash - ma - lon dos licht - l? Vos - zhe lust er mir tzu
stud - y. Does the can - dle have a mean - ing? Does it want to tell me

136

he - ren? S'ka - pet un es trift ir chay. - lev, Un s'vet bald fin ir nisht
some - thing? As it drips and melts its tal - low, Soon there will be naught re -

ve - ren. A - zoy tzank ich do in kley - zel, Vi a licht - l, shvach un
main - ing. Thus I sput - ter in the chap - el, Like the can - dle burn - ing

tin - kel, Biz ich vel a - zoy mir oys - geyn In der shtil in miz-rach vin - kel.
weak - ly, Till I too will be ex - tin-guished, Near the East Wall*, dy- ing meek - ly.

*East Wall—the wall of the synagogue along which sit the most highly priviledged.

137

SHLOF MAYN KIND, SHLOF KESEYDER
SLEEP MY CHILD, SLEEP SECURELY

Shlof mayn kind, ____ shlof ke - sey - der, Zin - gen vel ich
Sleep, my child, ____ sleep se - cure - ly, And I'll sing to

dir a lid. Az du mayn kind, ____ vest el - ter ve - rn,
you a song. When you, my child, ____ will grow to man - hood,

Ves - tu vi - sn an un - ter - shid. Az un - ter - shid.
You will learn to know right from wrong. When right from wrong.

Em   B7
Az du mayn kind, vest elter vern
 	
Em   Am
Vestu vern mit laytn glaych.
 	
   B7   Em B7 Em
Demolst vestu gevoyre vern
 	
B7   Em
Vost heyst orim uns vos heyst raych.   2
	Em B7
	When you, my child, will grow to manhood,
	
	Em Am
	There is one thing that is sure:
	
	   B7 Em B7 Em
	Then you'll see for yourself the great difference—
	
	B7 Em
	What is rich and what is poor. 2

Em   B7
Di tayrste palatsn, di shenste hayzer,
 	
Em   Am
Dos alts macht der oriman.
 	
   B7   Em B7 Em
Nor veystu ver es tut in zey voynen?
 	
B7   Em
Gor nisht er, nor der raycher man.   2
	Em B7
	The costly palace, the finest houses,
	
	Em Am
	Are all made by the workingman.
	
	   B7 Em B7 Em
	But do you know who lives within these mansions?
	
	B7 Em
	Never he—only rich folks can. 2

Em B7 Der oriman, er ligt in keler, Em Am Der vilgotsh rint im fun di vent. B7 Em B7 Em Derfun bakumt er a rematn-feler B7 Em In di fis un in di hent. 2	Em B7 The poor man's home is a dark cellar, Em Am Leaking, dripping, cold as sleet. B7 Em B7 Em And he is bound to get rheumatic fever, B7 Em Aches and pains in his hands and feet. 2

OT AZOY NEYT A SHNAYDER
STITCH AWAY, LITTLE TAILOR

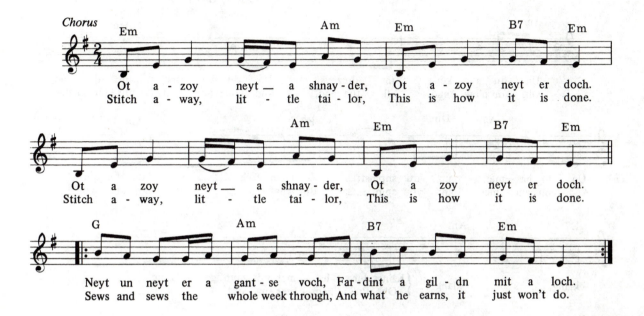

Ot a zoy neyt a shnay-der, Ot a zoy neyt er doch.
Stitch a - way, lit - tle tai - lor, This is how it is done.

Ot a zoy neyt a shnay-der, Ot a zoy neyt er doch.
Stitch a - way, lit - tle tai - lor, This is how it is done.

Neyt un neyt er a gant-se voch, Far-dint a gil-dn mit a loch.
Sews and sews the whole week through, And what he earns, it just won't do.

G   Am
A shnayder neyt un neyt un neyt,
 B7   Em
Fardint kadoches, nit kayn broyt. *Chorus*

G   Am
Farayorn, nit haynt gedacht,
 B7   Em
Hobn mir gehorevet fun acht biz acht. *Chorus*

G   Am
Ober di struktsye hot gemacht,
 B7   Em
Mir horeven shoyn mer nit fun acht biz acht. *Chorus*

G   Am
A tailor, he does sew and sew,
 B7   Em
Instead of bread, he earns just woe. *Chorus*

G   Am
A year ago—thank God it's done!
 B7   Em
We worked from dawn to setting sun. *Chorus*

G   Am
But since the union's come our way,
 B7   Em
We work no more a twelve-hour day. *Chorus*

UN DU AKERST
OH, YOU PLOW

Words by **CHAIM ZHITLOVSKY** (1865-1946)
Music Traditional

Am   **E7**
Zog vu iz dayn tish gegreyt,

    Am
Zog vu iz dayn yontef-kleyd.

    A7 Dm
Zog vu iz dayn sharfe shverd

E7   **Am**
Velechs glik iz dir bashert. *Chorus*

Am   **E7**
Man fun arbet, oyfgevacht!

    Am
Un derken dayn shtarke macht.

    A7 Dm
Ven dayn shtarke hant nor vil,

E7   **Am**
Shteyen ale reder shtil. *Chorus*

Am   **E7**
Say, where is your table laid,

    Am
And your dress for holiday.

    A7 Dm
Say, where is your sword of steel,

E7   **Am**
And what happiness you feel. *Chorus*

Am   **E7**
Workers of the world, unite!

    Am
You possess unbounded might.

    A7 Dm
It is up to your free will

E7   **Am**
If the wheels turn or stand still. *Chorus*

140

DIRE GELT
RENT MONEY

Em	Am
Kumt arayn der balabos,	Now here comes the landlord,

Em	Am
Mit dem grobn shtekn,	With his fancy cane.

Em	Am
Un az me git im kayn dire gelt,	And if you don't pay what is due,

B7	Em D7
Shtelt er aroys di betn. *Chorus & D. C.*	Eviction is his game. *Chorus & D. C.*

Em	Am
Farvos zol ich tsoln dire gelt,	Why do I have to pay rent?

Em	Am
Az di kich iz tsubrochn?	My kitchen is all broken.

Em	Am
Farvos zol ich gebn dire gelt	Why do I have to give him rent,

B7	Em D7
Az ich hob nisht af vos tsu kochn? *Chorus*	Since I cannot do my cooking? *Chorus*

Bozhe moy—Russian for "My God!"

Entrance to furniture dealer (meble), midwife (akuszerka), and dealer in railroad and train iron supplies (A. Stak), Warsaw, 1938. *(Courtesy Dr. Irving Levitas)*

BULBES
POTATOES

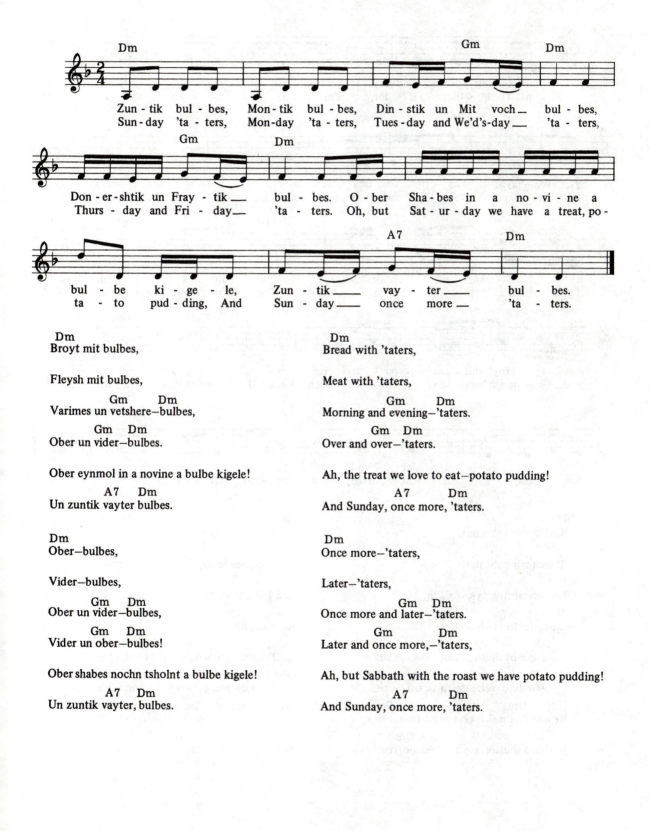

Zun - tik bul - bes, Mon - tik bul - bes, Din - stik un Mit voch __ bul - bes,
Sun - day 'ta - ters, Mon - day 'ta - ters, Tues - day and We'd's - day __ 'ta - ters,

Don - er - shtik un Fray - tik __ bul - bes. O - ber Sha - bes in a no - vi - ne a
Thurs - day and Fri - day __ 'ta - ters. Oh, but Sat - ur - day we have a treat, po -

bul - be ki - ge - le, Zun - tik __ vay - ter __ bul - bes.
ta - to pud - ding, And Sun - day __ once more __ 'ta - ters.

Dm Broyt mit bulbes,	Dm Bread with 'taters,
Fleysh mit bulbes,	Meat with 'taters,
Gm Dm Varimes un vetshere—bulbes,	Gm Dm Morning and evening—'taters.
Gm Dm Ober un vider—bulbes.	Gm Dm Over and over—'taters.
Ober eynmol in a novine a bulbe kigele!	Ah, the treat we love to eat—potato pudding!
A7 Dm Un zuntik vayter bulbes.	A7 Dm And Sunday, once more, 'taters.
Dm Ober—bulbes,	Dm Once more—'taters,
Vider—bulbes,	Later—'taters,
Gm Dm Ober un vider—bulbes,	Gm Dm Once more and later—'taters.
Gm Dm Vider un ober—bulbes!	Gm Dm Later and once more,—'taters,
Ober shabes nochn tsholnt a bulbe kigele!	Ah, but Sabbath with the roast we have potato pudding!
A7 Dm Un zuntik vayter, bulbes.	A7 Dm And Sunday, once more, 'taters.

BIN ICH MIR A SHNAYDERL
I'M A LITTLE TAILOR

Bin ich mir a shnay-der-l, Bin ich mir a shnay-der-l, Leb ich mir tog-
I'm a lit-tle tai-lor, I'm a lit-tle tai-lor, And I live from

oys, tog-ayn, Lus-tig un frey-lech un fayn. Zog mir, shnay-der,
day to day, Jol-ly and hap-py and gay. Tell me, tai-lor,

li-bin-ker un gu-ter. Git dir di no-dl, ge-
if the truth you ut-ter, Does your fine nee-dle give

nug oyf broyt mit pu-ter? Ich mach a voch, tsvey gil-dn mit a
you e-nough bread and but-ter? Each week I earn a bare hand-ful of

dray-er, Ich es nor broyt, vayl pu-ter iz tsu tay-er.
pen-nies, I eat just bread, but but-ter have-n't an-y.

Dm Bin ich mir a shusterl,	**Dm** I'm a little cobbler,
Bin ich mir a shusterl,	I'm a little cobbler,
C **F** Leb ich mir tog oys, tog ayn,	**C** **F** And I live from day to day,
Dm **A7** **Dm** Lustig un freylech un fayn,	**Dm** **A7** **Dm** Jolly and happy and gay.
F Zog mir, shuster, hostu vos tsu kayen?	**F** Tell me, cobbler, is there food a-plenty?
Dm Felt dir oyset, krigstu vu tsu layen?	**Dm** What do you eat—is your stomach empty?
Bb **Dm** **Gm** **Dm** Keyner layt nisht, keyner git kayn orves,	**Bb** **Dm** **Gm** **Dm** No one helps me, no one gives me credit.
G **Dm** Ich bin a shuster, gey ich take borves.	**G** **Dm** As for my own shoes—I have to forget it.

```
Dm
Bin ich mir a blecherl,

Bin ich mir a blecherl,
               C       F
Leb ich mir tog oys, tog ayn,
Dm      A7      Dm
Lustig un freylech un fayn.
      F
   Zog mir, blecher, vi groys iz bay dir di noyt?
  Dm
   Hostu bulkes, hostu nit kayn broyt?
 Bb     Dm     Gm        Dm
Ich zits un klap bay yenem fremde decher,
             G      Dm
Bay mir in shtub rint fun ale lecher.


Dm
Bin ich mir a kremerl,

Bin ich mir a kremerl,
               C       F
Leb ich mir tog oys, tog ayn,
Dm      A7      Dm
Lustig un freylech un fayn.
      F
   Zog mir, kremer, tsu hostu mit vos tsu handlen?
  Dm
   Hostu in kreml rozhinkes mit mandlen?
 Bb     Dm  Gm         Dm
Ich hob in kreml far tsvey groshn schoyne,
             G                Dm
Ich shlep dem dalis, un ich bentsch dem boyse.
```

```
Dm
I'm a little tinsmith,

I'm a little tinsmith,
               C       F
And I live from day to day,
Dm      A7      Dm
Jolly and happy and gay.
      F
   Tell me, tinsmith, how great is your need?
  Dm
   Have you bread and rolls, your family to feed?
 Bb     Dm     Gm        Dm
I fix others' roofs for days and for weeks,
                        G      Dm
While in my own room the old ceiling leaks.


Dm
I'm a little merchant,

I'm a little merchant,
               C       F
And I live from day to day,
Dm      A7      Dm
Jolly and happy and gay.
       F
   Tell me, merchant, what have you in your store?
  Dm
   Raisins and almonds—have you any more?
 Bb     Dm     Gm          Dm
I have in my store two cents' worth of sorrow.
             G          Dm
All I can do is worry 'bout tomorrow.
```

(above) The author's paternal grandfather, Israel Silverman (left), in the
1890s, and the author's children Antoine and David in 1977 (below).

VI ZENEN MAYNE YUNGE YOREN?
WHERE ARE MY YOUTHFUL YEARS?

Freely

Vi ze - nen, ___ may - ne yun - ge yo - ren? ___ Vi ze -
Where are they, ___ all my youth - ful years? _____ Where are

nen may - ne tsay - ten? ___ Ich hob ___ far - shpilt ___
they, all the good _____ times? ___ I've gam - bled a - way ___

may - ne yun - ge yo - ren, A - zoy vi men shpilt ___ in kor - ten. _____
all my youth-ful years, As if they were lost ___ in card games. _____

Em **G** Un az men tit in korten shpilen,	**Em** **G** When you lose in playing cards,
Em Am Em Shpilt men doch in gelt.	**Em Am Em** Gold is all the cost.
A Am **Em** Un ich hob farshpilt mayne yunge yoren	**A Am** **Em** I've gambled away all my youthful years,
Am **B7** **Em** Un dertsi mayne sheyne velt.	**Am** **B7** **Em** And with them my world is lost.
Em **G** Zaprihayte, brati, koni,	**Em** **G** Brothers, let our horses gallop,
Em Am Em Koni voroni—	**Em Am** **Em** Steeds of raven-black.
A Am Em Dohonaymo nashi lyati,	**A Am** **Em** Let us chase our youthful years,
Am B7 Em Lyati molodi.*	**Am** **B7** **Em** Years that never can come back.

*This verse is in Ukrainian.

147

Amerike! Amerike!

"Americanized" in the early 1920s.

LIDL FUN GOLDENEM LAND
SONG OF THE GOLDEN LAND

When Tsar Alexander II was assassinated by revolutionary terrorists on March 1, 1881, the modest attempts at liberalism vis-à-vis the Russian Jews came to an abrupt end. With the accession of Alexander III came a wave of bloody pogroms and persecutions that set into motion a new and monumental exodus.

The first Jewish immigrants had arrived in the Dutch colony of New Amsterdam as early as 1654. Over the intervening two centuries a slow trickle of Jews (some 7,500 between 1820 and 1850, for example) had made their way to the New World. By the 1870s that trickle had grown substantially, as over 40,000 new arrivals were counted. Emigration up to that point was, however, a decision prompted by individual desire. The reign of terror of Alexander III changed all that. Now it became literally a question of collective survival.

America, "The Golden Land," took on mythic proportions in the minds of the Jewish masses. One expression of this new consciousness was formed in poetry and song . . .

See note on page 184.

By **MORDECHAI GEBIRTIG**

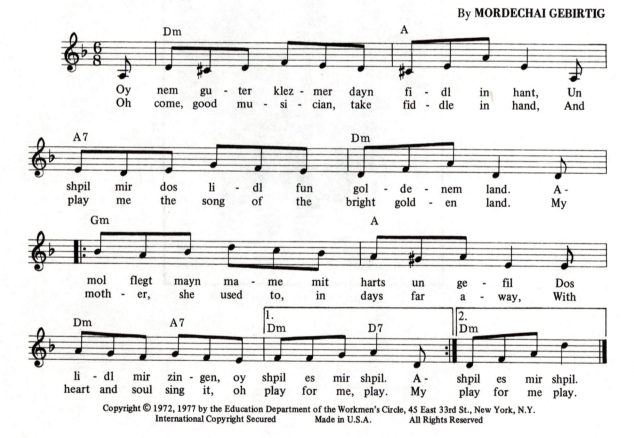

Dm   A
Un her ich dos lidl dan shvebt far mir bald,
    A7   Dm
Mayn tayere mame, ir liblech geshtalt.
   Gm   A
Ir hartsiker shmeychl, ir tsertlecher blik,
   Dm   A7   Dm   D7
Zey vekn mir oyf mayn fargangenem glik.
   Gm   A
Ir hartsiker shmeychl, ir tsertlecher blik,
   Dm   A7   Dm
Zey vekn mir oyf mayn fargangenem glik.

Dm   A
Un her ich dos lidl, derze ich, ot shteyt
    A7   Dm
Mayn mame, zi macht mir mayn vigele greyt.
   Gm   A
Un ch'fil oyf mayn shtern ir darinke hant,
   Dm   A7   Dm   D7
Zi zingt mir dos lidl fun goldenem land.
   Gm   A
Un ch'fil oyf mayn shtern ir darinke hant,
   Dm   A7   Dm
Zi zingt mir dos lidl fun goldenem land.

   Dm   A
"Amol iz geven in a goldenem land,
    A7   Dm
A kluger ben yochid, a sheyner brilyant."
   Gm   A
Zi zingt un es tiktakt dem zeygers umru,
   Dm A7   Dm   D7
Un s'vigele hoydet zich, "Ay lu lu lu."
   Gm   A
Zi zingt un es tiktakt dem zeygers umru.
   Dm A7   Dm
Un s'vigele hoydet zich, "Ay lu lu lu."

Dm   A
And when I do hear it, then it seems to me
   A7   Dm
I see my dear mama as she used to be.
   Gm   A
Her lovely face smiling, her twinkling eye,
   Dm   A7   Dm   D7
They rouse in my thoughts happy days long gone by.
   Gm   A
Her lovely face smiling, her twinkling eye,
   Dm   A7   Dm
They rouse in my thoughts happy days long gone by.

   Dm   A
And when I do hear it, I see how she stands,
    A7   Dm
And makes up my cradle with her loving hands.
   Gm   A
I feel on my temple her delicate hand.
   Dm   A7   Dm   D7
She sings me the chorus of the golden land.
   Gm   A
I feel on my temple her delicate hand.
   Dm   A7   Dm
She sings me the chorus of the golden land.

    Dm   A
"There was long ago in a bright golden land,
    A7   Dm
A clever young scholar, a brilliant young man."
   Gm   A
She sings and the clock ticks; the hours fly by.
   Dm   A7   Dm   D7
The cradle rocks back and forth—"Oh, hush-a-bye."
   Gm   A
She sings and the clock ticks; the hours fly by.
   Dm   A7   Dm
The cradle rocks back and forth—"Oh, hush-a-bye."

דער אַרבעטער־רינג
פּרעזענטירט
דאָס גאָלדענע לאַנד
צונויפֿגעגעשטעלט, געשריבן און רעזשיסירט פֿון
זלמן מלאָטעק און משה ראָזנפֿעלד

The Workmen's Circle

Presents

THE GOLDEN LAND
A musical montage in two acts,
compiled, written and directed by
ZALMEN MLOTEK and MOISHE ROSENFELD

SHIKT A TIKET
SEND A TICKET

This poignant appeal for passage to America ends with a realistic warning about the difficulties of passing through U.S. immigration inspection at Castle Garden. Immigrants had begun to be processed in 1855 in this fort which was built in 1807 on a small island near the west side of the Battery. By the 1880s the outdated structure clearly could not accommodate the thousands of immigrants who arrived each week. In 1892 Ellis Island was dedicated as the main immigration center. Castle Garden was joined to the Battery by a landfill—but the memories remained.

In Rus - land gants vayt, dort vart a - za tsayt, Ayn or - e - me fa - mil - ye on shir._____ Zey der - var - tn a - tsind, fun A - mer - i - ke ge - shvind, Dem ant - vort dos shti - ke - le pa - pir. _____ Zey shray - bn tsu a fraynt, "Es iz di tsayt shlecht haynt, Po - gro - men un tso - res on tsol; _____

In Rus - sia, so far, the land of the tsar, A fam - i - ly that's poor with - out end,_____ In great an - guish they wait, be - fore it's too____ late, The an - swer A - mer - i - ca will send._____ They write____ to a friend, "Our trou - bles nev - er end, Po - groms and af - flic - tions per - sist;_____

Da - rum be - tn mir aych, shikt a ti - ket glaych; Far -
So we will make this vow, send a tick - et now, We

ge - sn ve - ln mir aych keyn - mol." Ba - tracht nor a -
nev - er will for - get you for this." Just think, my dear

tsind, in Ke - sl Gar - dn ge - shvind, Vi - fil tre - rn gi - sn zich
friend of that place, Cas - tle Gar - den, All the tears that peo - ple shed

dort, Un ver es hot keyn glik, dem shikt men tsu -
there, And he who has no luck, they send him right

rik, Tsu - rik oyf dem um - glik - le - chn ort.
back, Right back to the land of great de - spair.

Libau, Latvia, a port on the Baltic, as it looked in 1913.
Many Russian Jewish emigrants took ship here for England, and eventually to America.

153

EYN ZACH VEL ICH
ONE THING I ASK

During the 1880s many Jews in Eastern Europe believed the rumors that slavery still existed in the United States. Nevertheless, the hardships under the tsar were so terrible that the singer in this song—expressing what must have been a widespread feeling—is willing even to endure slavery in the United States rather than continuing to live in Russia.

Eyn zach vel ich Got bay dir be - tn, az di
On - ly one thing I ask of you ___ God, and I

zach ___ zol mir zayn ___ ba - shert; Fun Rus - land muz ich op -
hope ___ it will be ___ my ___ fate; From Rus - sia I must de -

tre - tn, keyn A - mer - i - ke vet zayn ___ mayn pa - chod. Fun
part ___ now, To A - mer - i - ca I now ___ turn, my gait. I

key - ne gli - kn veys ich ___ nit, in Rus - land iz mir zey - er shlecht.
know no hap - pi - ness at ___ all, in Rus - sia things are ver - y grave.

Kayn A - mer - i - ke muz ich op - fo - rn, far -
For A - mer - i - ca I have to leave now, to

koy - fn vel ich zich far a knecht.
sell my - self as a low - ly slave.

154

FRAYHAYT STATUE
STATUE OF LIBERTY

By ABRAHAM LIESSIN
and L. WEINER

O kumt ir far - vo - gel - te, O kumt ir ge - drik - te, Fun
Oh come you op - press - éd ones, Oh come, bent and bro - ken, Weighed

vel - - tn ge - pak - te, Fun vel - tn far - shtik - te A -
down ___ by your bur - dens, The world that has choked you, And

her in di vay - tn an end. Kumt tsu di bra - ve
see in the dis - tance an end. Come to the brave, ___

Kumt tsu di fray - e, Ir vet zich mit koy - ches Do on - ne - men
Come to the free, ___ We'll give you new cour - age, Just you wait and

nay - e, Mir gi - bn aych har - tsik di hent. hent.
see, We heart - i - ly give you our hand. hand.

155

KESL GARDN
CASTLE GARDEN

Morris Rosenfeld, who came to be known as the poet of the sweatshop, himself entered New York through Castle Garden in 1886. He, and thousands of immigrants like him, were ill prepared for the chaotic conditions at Castle Garden, and for the dehumanizing life of the sweatshop "once you pass the door."

Words by **MORRIS ROSENFELD** (1862-1923)
Music by **MARK WARSHAWSKY**

Mit vey un shmerts Vert i-ber-filt mayn harts Ven ich gib oyf Ke-sl
My heart with pain Does o-ver-flow a-gain, When at Cas-tle Gar-den

Gar-dn a blik._____ Vu ment-shen mil-yo-nen Fun far-
I give a glance._____ Where folks of all sta-tions From so

shi-de-ne nats-yo-nen Zi-tsn un troy-men fun glik._____
man-y dif-f'rent na-tions Sit dream-ing of bet-ter chance._____

Ch'-denk es oyf klor, Tsu-rik mit acht yor,_____ Bin
I re-mem-ber it so, Just eight years a-go._____ That

ich dort ge-ze-sn a-leyn._____ Ge-hoft un ge-lacht, Fun
I sat a-lone in that place;_____ A hope-ful young boy, I

glik nor ge-tracht, Vi gut iz mir de-molst ge-ven,_____ In
thought of my joy, The hap-pi-ness shone in my face,_____ In

156

Ke - sl Gar - dn, Oyf ye - ner zayt tir, Ge - fint mir dem
Cas - tle Gar - den, Once you pass the door, The grave of my

grub fun mayn glik, _____ Un noch fi - le kvo - rim A
joy you will see, _____ And sim - i - lar tombs You will

zel - che on shir, Ge - fint ir vu ir git nor a blik. _____
find more and more, Wher - ev - er you may look, be - lieve me. _____

E	**Dm6**	**E**	**Dm6**
Doch gibn mir tsu		But nevertheless,	
E	**Dm6**	**E**	**Dm6**
Az frayhayt un ru,		Of freedom and rest,	
E	**Am**	**E**	**E Am E**
Hobn mir do mer vi iberal.		We have here more than elsewhere.	

Fun libe un fridn, (Dm6)
For love and peace, too, (Dm6)

Far kristn un yidn, (E Dm6)
For Gentile and Jew, (E Dm6)

Tsaygt zich undz do yetst a shtral. (E Dm E)
A ray of hope shines in the air. (E Dm E)

Nor nemt oych in acht (Dm E)
But do have a care, (Dm E)

Nit farshlept do di nacht, (Dm E Am)
And leave over there (Dm E Am)

Di finsternish der altn velt; (G F E)
The darkness that we knew of old. (G F E)

Di heymishe sam (A#dim E7)
The old misery, (A#dim E7)

Lozt zinken in yam, (A#dim Bm)
Let it sink in the sea, (A#dim Bm)

Un do zet, nit shecht zich far gelt. (G F E)
And don't kill yourself just for gold. (G F E)

Dan vet Kesl Gardn (E7 Am)
Then will Castle Garden (E7 Am)

A lust gortn zayn, (E7)
A joyous place be, (E7)

Un aych vet men shetsn in land; (Am Dm E)
And people will honor its name. (Am Dm E)

Dan vet men aych yidn (E7 Am)
Then will all Jews finally (E7 Am)

Bahandlen do fayn (Dm6 E)
Feel that they're free, (Dm6 E)

Farshvundn vet dumhayt un shand. (Am Dm6 E)
And vanish will ignorance and shame. (Am Dm6 E)

157

LEBN ZOL KOLOMBUS
LONG LIFE TO COLUMBUS

Coming from the nineteenth-century Yiddish theater in America, this rambunctious music-hall number expressed the immigrant's joy in his new life. Christopher Columbus was a common symbol for the good *and* bad encountered in America.

By A. PERLMUTTER
and H. WOHL

A shte - tl iz A - me - ri - ke, A me - chay - e chle - bn; Es
A - mer - i - ca's a hap - py place, Real - ly, what a trea - sure. You'll

rut oyf ir di shchi - ne - le Mir zo - ln a - zoy le - bn. Mil -
see it plain on ev - 'ry face, There's noth - ing here but plea - sure. For

cho - mes, bik - sn, men - tshn blut Dar - fn mir oyf tso - res, A
wars and guns and shed - ding blood, No - bod - y does need them, A

gu - ber - na - tor darf men nit, A key - ser oyf ka - po - res.
gov - er - nor, and a tsar, too, Oh nev - er - more to heed them.

Faster

Ay, siz gut, zingt zhe a - le mit: Oy, le - bn zol Ko - lum - bus, trinkt
Ah, it's good, sing this song with me: Oh, long life to Co - lum - bus, my

bri - der - lech le - cha - yim. Le - bn zol Ko - lum - bus, oy
broth - ers drink this toast. Long life to Co - lum - bus, this

far dem land dem nay - im. Zayt tsu - fri - dn, gleybt nit in di trom - bes;
land from coast to coast. All be hap - py, don't let wise guys fool us;

Shrayt zhe yi - dn: Le - bn zol Ko - lum - bus, le - bn zol Ko - lum - bus!
Ev - 'ry Jew shouts: Long life to Co - lum - bus, long life to Co - lum - bus!

KOLOMBUS, ICH HOB TSU DIR GORNIT
COLUMBUS, I GIVE YOU THE FIRST PRIZE

By D. MEYOROWITZ

ELIS AYLAND
ELLIS ISLAND

"All passenger vessels are boarded at Quarantine by inspectors from the Immigration Bureau . . . and if any passenger is thought to be a person who comes within the restrictive clauses of the law he is compelled to go to Ellis Island and await investigation. . . . As an instance of the care that is exercised to prevent improper persons from landing, statistics show that as many as 800 immigrants have been detained and returned to their homes in Italy in one month." — *The New York Times,* January 31, 1897.

O El - is Ay - land, Du gre - nets fun fray - land, Vi groys un vi
O El - lis Is - land, You bor - der of free land, How big and how

shrek - lech du bist! ___ A - zel - che r' - tsi - ches Dos
fear - ful you are! ___ You vis - it such crimes With - out

ke - nen nor ru - ches, Du plagst di ge - plag - te um - zist, ___ Mit
rea - son or rhyme On the peo - ple who come from a - far, ___ With

tso - res ge - ku - men, Dem yam koym der - shvu - men Di ge - tin der
great - est e - mo - tion, They've just crossed the o - cean, And seen free - dom's

fray - hayt der - zen. ___ Do kumt ___ El - lis Ay - land, Der
god - dess on high. ___ But cruel ___ El - is Is - land, The

gre - nets fun fray - land, Zogt, "Halt, du kenst vay - ter nit geyn." ___
bor - der of free land, Says, "Halt, you can nev - er pass by." ___

NEW YORKER TRERN
THE TEARS OF NEW YORK

Annie P., 44 Allen Street, front tenement, second floor. Husband Louis P. came here three years ago and one year ago sent for wife and three children. From that time unfortunately, his trade, that of shoemaker, became less remunerative. She helped by washing and like labor, but two months ago he deserted her, though she stoutly maintains he returned to Odessa to get his old work back. The youngest, Meyer P., age five years, fell from the table and injured his hip. He lay for 7 months in the Orthopedic Hospital, 42nd Street; he was discharged as incurable and supplied with a brace . . . The mother is absolutely tied by her pregnant condition; the cripple is in pain and cries to be carried. They had no rooms of their own but paid $3 a month to Hannah A., a decent tailoress, who allowed the family to sleep on her floor . . . Sunday I saw them. Monday I filed application with Montefiore Home for Meyer's admission . . . Tuesday I went to Hebrew Sheltering Guardian Society, saw Superintendent, and obtained promise of place for the two well children by Thursday . . . Thursday afternoon we washed and dressed the two children, and I left them in the afternoon at the Asylum, leaving my address for the Superintendent so that he might know their friend in case of need. They have absolutely no one in America but their mother.

—From a letter by Lillian Wald, the founder of the Henry Street Settlement, to the philanthropist Jacob Schiff, 1893.

By **H. ALTMAN**

Slowly

Em — Am — Em

Ot dos zay - nen di New York - er tre - rn, Vos
O, now these are the New York - er's tears, — Which

Am

ke - nen keyn - mol nit oyf he - rn, A krechts,
con - stant - ly sound in your ears, A shout,

B7 — Em — C

a ge - shrey, a zifts un a vey, Dos kent ir nor
and a moan, a sigh and a groan, And that is the

F#7 — B7 — Em

i - mer do he - rn. Dos iz shoyn nit nay, Vu ir
sound that one hears. The old tale of woe, Wher

Am — B7 — Em

geyt nor far - bay Zet ir di New York - er tre - rn.
ev - er you go, You'll see the New York - er's tears.

EYDER ICH LEYG MICH SHLOFN
NO SOONER DO I LIE DOWN

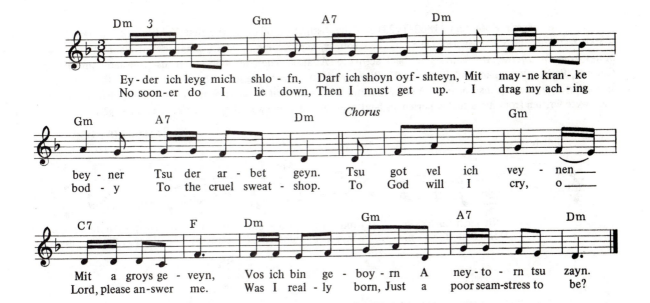

Ey-der ich leyg mich shlo - fn, Darf ich shoyn oyf - shteyn, Mit may - ne kran - ke
No soon-er do I lie down, Then I must get up. I drag my ach - ing

bey - ner Tsu der ar - bet geyn. Tsu got vel ich vey - nen
bod - y To the cruel sweat - shop. To God will I cry, o

Mit a groys ge - veyn, Vos ich bin ge - boy - rn A ney - to - rn tsu zayn.
Lord, please an - swer me. Was I real - ly born, Just a poor seam - stress to be?

Dm   Gm
Ch'kum shpet tsu der arbet

A7   Dm
S'iz doch vayt der veg,

Gm
Shlogt men mir op

A7   Dm
Far halbe teg. *Chorus*

Dm   Gm
Di nodlen vern tsubrochn

A7   Dm
Fuftsn a menut.

Gm
Di finger vern tsushtochn,

A7   Dm
Es rint fun zey dos blut. *Chorus*

Dm   Gm
Ich layd shtendig hunger

A7   Dm
Ich hob nit vos tsu esn.

Gm
Vil ich gelt betn,

A7   Dm
Heyst men mir fargesn. *Chorus*

Dm   Gm
If I'm late to work,

A7   Dm
Since I live far away,

Gm
Then I am docked,

A7   Dm
Docked a half-day's pay. *Chorus*

Dm   Gm
The needles, they get broken,

A7   Dm
Fifteen at a time.

Gm
Our fingers, they are bleeding—

A7   Dm
It's a dirty crime. *Chorus*

Dm   Gm
I am always hungry,

A7   Dm
With not enough to eat.

Gm
If I ask for more money—

A7   Dm
I'm out on the street. *Chorus*

MAYN RUE PLATS
MY RESTING PLACE

Morris Rosenfeld (1862–1923) has the distinction of being the first Yiddish poet to have had his works translated into English (in 1898, by Leo Weiner, a professor of Slavic languages at Harvard University: *Songs from the Ghetto*). His fame spread back across the Atlantic, where his works were also translated into French, German, Polish, Bohemian, and Russian (the Russian edition was brought out by Maxim Gorki). He even made a European tour, reading his poems in Yiddish to enthusiastic audiences. His poems are all the more stirring because they were written from his actual experiences bent over machines in sweatshops and as a union delegate.

By **MORRIS ROSENFELD**

Nit zuch mich vu di mir - tn grin - en. Ge - finst mich dor - tn nit, mayn shats. Vu le - bens vel - kn bay ma - shi - nen; Dor - tn iz mayn ru - e plats, Dor - tn iz mayn ru - e plats.

Don't look for me where myr - tles blos - som. Dear, there you'll nev - er see my face. Where lives are wast - ed in the fac - t'ry; There you'll find my rest - ing place, There you'll find my rest - ing place.

Am		C	Am
Nit zuch mich vu di feygl zingen.

| | C | E7 | Am |
Gefinst mich dortn nit, mayn shats.

| | | C | |
A shklaf bin ich, vu keytn klingen;

| D#dim G7 | | C | |
Dortn iz mayn rue plats,

| E7 Am Dm | D#dim E7 Am | | |
Dortn iz mayn ru - e plats.

Am		C	Am
Don't look for me where birds are singing,

| | C | E7 | Am |
Dear, there you'll never see my face.

| | | C | |
A slave am I where chains are ringing;

| D#dim | G7 | C | |
There you'll find my resting place,

| E7 | Am Dm D#dim E7 Am | | |
There you'll find my rest - ing place.

164

Am   C   Am
    Nit zuch mich vu fontanen shpritsn.

         C   E7   Am
    Gefinst mich dortn nit, mayn shats.

                 C
    Vu trern rinen, tseyner kritsn;

D♯dim G7   C
    Dortn iz mayn rue plats,

  E7 Am Dm D♯dim E7 Am
    Dortn iz   mayn ru - e plats.

Am   C   Am
    Un libstu mich mit varer libe,

         C   E7   Am
    To kum tsu mir mayn guter shats,

                C
    Un hayter oyf mayn harts dos tribe,

  D♯dim   G7   C
    Un mach mir zis mayn rue plats,

    E7   Am Dm D♯dim E7 Am
    Un mach mir zis   mayn ru - e plats.

Am   C   Am
    Don't look for me 'mong fountains splashing,

         C   E7   Am
    Dear, there you'll never see my face.

                     C
    Where tears are flowing, teeth are gnashing;

D♯dim   G7   C
    There you'll find my resting place,

    E7   Am Dm D♯dim E7 Am
    There you'll find my rest - ing place.

Am   C   Am
    And if your love is truly burning,

         C   E7   Am
    Then come to me in fond embrace,

                 C
    And put an end to all my yearning,

    D♯dim   G7   C
    And make it sweet—my resting place,

     E7   Am Dm D♯dim E7 Am
    And make it sweet — my rest - ing place.

Thompsonville, New York, 1925

MAYN YINGELE
MY LITTLE SON

When Morris Rosenfeld wrote the words to this song in New York in 1887, the immigration of Eastern European Jews was gaining momentum. Hoping for a "golden land," many found the unbearable life of the sweatshop instead. So it was with Rosenfeld himself, who here describes his real feelings about his real son.

Ich hob a kley-nem yin-ge-le, A zu-ne-le gor fayn. Ven
I have a lit-tle ba-by boy, A lit-tle boy so fine. And

ich der-ze im dacht zich mir, Di gan-tse velt iz mayn. Nor
when I look at him, it seems The whole wide world is mine. But

zel-tn, zel-tn ze ich im, Mayn shey-nem ven er vacht. Ich
sel-dom, sel-dom do I see My son when he's a-wake. I

tref im i-mer shlof-n-dig, Ich ze im nor bay nacht.
see him al-ways sleep-ing, It's hard for me to take.

Em B(7)	Em B(7)
Di arbet traybt mich fri aroys,	It's early when I go to work,
Am B7	Am B7
Un lozt mich shpet tsurik.	It's late when work is done.
Em	Em
O, fremd, iz mir mayn eygn kind,	Why is it—tell me, must I be
Am6	Am6
O, fremd, mayn kind's a blik.	A stranger to my son?
B7 Em	B7 Em
Ich kum tsuklemterheyt aheym,	I drag myself, exhausted, home,
C Am6	C Am6
In finsternish gehilt,	When darkness starts to fall.
B7 Em	B7 Em
Mayn bleyche froy dertseylt mir bald	My pale wife tells me of our son,
Am B	Am B
Vi fayn dos kind zich shpilt.	How he's the best of all.

166

Em   B(7)
Vi zis es redt, vi klug es fregt:

Am   B7
"O Mame, gute Ma,

Em
Ven kumt un brengt a pene mir,

Am6
Mayn guter, guter pa?"

B7   Em
Ich her es tsu, un yo, es muz,

C   Am6
Yo, yo, es muz geshen!

B7   Em
Di foter-libe flakert oyf,

Am   B
Es muz mayn kind mich zen!

Em   B(7)
Ich shtey bay zayn gelegerl,

Am   B7
Un ze un her un sha;

Em
A troym bavegt di lipelech:

Am6
"O, vu iz, vu iz pa."

B7   Em
Ich kush di bloye oygelech,

C   Am6
Zey efenen zich, O kind!

B7   Em
Zey zeyen mich, zey zeyen mich!

Am   B
Un shlisn zich geshvind.

Em   B(7)
Do shteyt dayn papa tayerer,

Am   B7
A penele dir, na!

Em
A troym bavegt di lipelech;

Am6
"O vu iz, vu iz pa?"

B7   Em
Ich blayb tsuveytogt un tsuklemt,

C   Am6
Farbitert, un ich kler:

B7   Em
"Ven du ervachst amol, mayn kind,

Am   B
Gefinstu mich nit mer."

Em   B(7)
He sweetly speaks, he brightly asks,

Am   B7
"Oh, Mama, dearest Ma,

Em
When he comes home will I receive

Am6
A penny from Papa?"

B7   Em
I hear her tale, and, yes, I swear,

C   Am6
I swear that it must be!

B7   Em
True father-love burns in my heart,

Am   B
My son, his dad must see!

Em   B(7)
I stand beside his little crib,

Am   B7
And listen quietly.

Em
He has a dream—his lips, they move;

Am6
"Oh, where is my daddy?"

B7   Em
I kiss his little eyes of blue.

C   Am6
They open. Oh, my son!

B7   Em
They look at me, they look at me!

Am   B
Then quickly close again.

Em   B(7)
Here is your father, full of love.

Am   B7
A penny—take it—here!

Em
He has a dream—his lips, they move:

Am6
"Where is my daddy dear?"

B7   Em
In sorrow and in pain I stand,

C   Am6
Embittered, and I say,

B7   Em
"When you awake again, my child,

Am   B
Your dad will be away."

SVETSHOP
SWEATSHOP

In the decade between 1880 and 1890, 5,246,613 immigrants entered the United States. Among them, in 1881, was David Edelstadt, who came to America at the age of fifteen after escaping the terrible Kiev pogrom of May 8, 1881. He found employment in sweatshops and subsequently contracted tuberculosis. Because of his personal tragedy he was able to express in his poetry the sentiments of the exploited immigrant worker. He died in 1892 at the age of twenty-six.

By **DAVID EDELSTADT**
(1866-1892)

With movement

Shnel___ loy - fn di re - der, Vild___ kla - pn ma - shi - nen, In
Wheels___ turn - ing so swift - ly, Wild - ly pound-ing ma - chin-er - y, The

shop iz shmu - tsik un heys.___ Der kop vert far - tu - mlt In
shop is dir - ty and hot.___ My head, how it's ach - ing, My

oy - gn vert fin - ster, Fin - ster fun trern ___ un shveys. Der
eyes see but dark - ness, Dark - ness from tears ___ and sweat. My

kop vert far - tu - mlt In oy - gn vert fin - ster, Fin - ster fun trern ___ un shveys.
head, how it's ach - ing, My eyes see but dark-ness, Dark - ness from tears ___ and sweat.

Em
Ich fil shoyn bay zich
      D7 G
Kayn gantsn eyver;
  Am   D7   Gsus4 G
Tsebrokhn, tsedrikt iz mayn brust;
     C   B7
Ich ken shoyn far veytok
    Am   C
Mayn rukn nit boygn,
  D7   G D7   B7
Banacht lozt nit shlofn der hust.
    C   B7
Ich ken shoyn far veytok
   Am   C
Mayn rukn nit boygn,
Amsus4 Am   B7   Em
Banacht lozt nit shlofn der hust.

   Em
Loyft um der mayster,
   D7 G
A khaye, a vilde,
   Am   D7   Gsus4 G
Er traybt tsu der sh'chite di shof;
    C   B7
O, vi lang vet ir vartn,
   Am   C
Vi lang vet ir duldn?
 D7   G D7   B7
Arbeter brider, vacht oyf!
    C   B7
O, vi lang vet ir vartn,
   Am   C
Vi lang vet ir duldn?
Amsus4 Am B7   Em
  Arbeter brider, vacht oyf!

Em
It just seems to me
     D7 G
That I'm torn to pieces.
  Am   D7   Gsus4 G
Broken and bent is my breast.
    C   B7
The pain is so bad
     Am   C
That I can't bend my back,
    D7   G D7   B7
And coughing at night robs my rest.
    C   B7
The pain is so bad
    Am   C
That I can't bend my back,
  Amsus4 Am B7   Em
And coughing at night robs my rest.

Em
All around runs the foreman,
    D7 G
A beast, a wild one.
  Am   D7   Gsus4 G
He drives to the slaughter the sheep.
     C   B7
Oh, how long will you wait,
   Am   C
How long to be patient?
    D7   G D7   B7
Wake up, working brother, don't sleep!
    C   B7
Oh, how long will you wait,
   Am   C
How long to be patient?
  Amsus4 Am   B7   Em
Wake up, working brother, don't sleep!

DEM PEDLERS BRIVL
THE PEDDLER'S LETTER

The neighborhood of Hester, Norfolk, and Essex Streets presents a quaint scene. The streets are black with purchasers, and bright with the glare of hundreds of torches from the pushcarts. The . . . voices of the peddlers crying their wares, the expostulations of the purchasers, the mingling of the "Yiddish" of the elders with the English of the young people, make a strange medley of sounds. . . . It is estimated that there are 1,500 peddlers of various wares in that vicinity. The regular peddler pays $25 a year for his license with additional fees to the police. He can hardly earn more than $5 a week so he often hires a pushcart for his wife, and sometimes the children too are brought into the service. The rent of a pushcart is 10 cents a day. Many of the peddlers are only temporarily in the trade. Tailors or mechanics who are out of work hire a pushcart until they find a position. Recently landed immigrants are advised by their friends to take a pushcart until they can establish themselves in some business.

—New York Tribune, September 15, 1898

By **Y. BRISKER**

O, tay - e - re ma - me, du fregst mir vos mach ich, Du
O, my dear - est Ma - ma, you ask how I'm do - ing, You

fregst vos ich tu do in gol - den - em land.___ Ich ken dir nit, ma - mi - she,
ask what I do here in this gol - den land.___ I can - not write, Ma - ma dear,

shray - bn keyn li - gn,___ Un shray - bn dem e - mes ot tsi - tert___ mayn
lies in my let - ter,___ So I'll write the truth with a trem - bl - ing

hant. Ich ken dir nit, ma - mi - she, shray - bn keyn li - gn,___ Un
hand. I can - not write, Ma - ma dear, lies in my let - ter,___ So

shray - bn dem e - mes ot tsi - tert mayn hant.___ Ich pe - dl, ich pe - dl a-
I'll write the truth with a trem - bl - ing hand.___ I ped - dle, I ped - dle in

rum i - ber di hay - zer, Nish - to keyn tsu vayt, _ nish - to keyn tsu hoych. __ In
all of the big hous - es, Not one is too far, _ not one is too tall. __ In

hits un in kelt un in vint un in re - gn, ___ Men shlept zich, men loyft mi - tn
heat and in cold and in wind and in rain - storm, __ We creep and we run till ex-

letst bi - sl koy - ach. In hits un in kelt un in vint un in re - gn, __
haust - ed __ we fall. __ In heat and in cold and in wind and in rain - storm,_

Men shlept zich, men loyft mi - tn letst bi - sl koy - ach. __
We creep and we run till ex - haust - ed we fall. __

ARBETER FROYEN
YOU WORKING WOMEN

By DAVID EDELSTADT

Ar - be - ter froy - en, lay - den - de froy - en,
You work - ing wom - en, suf - fer - ing wom - en,

Froy - en vos shmach - tn in hoyz un fab - rik; Vos shteyt ir fun
Wom - en who lan - guish at home and in mills; Oh, why don't you

vay - tn, vos helft ir nit boy - en Dem tem - pl fun
help___ us in build - ing the tem - ple Of free - dom and

fray - hayt, fun mentsh - le - chn glik? Helft undz tro - gn dem
joy that will end the world's ills? Help us car - ry the

ba - ner, dem roy - tn For - verts durch shturm,___ durch fin - ste - re
ban - ner of scar - let For - ward through storm___ and through the dark

necht. Helft undz var - hayt ___ un licht tsu far - shprey - tn,
night. Help us bring truth___ to all of the peo - ple,

Tsvi - shn um - vi - sn - de e - ln - de knecht.___
To the un - for - tu - nate let us bring light.___

Em   B7
Helft undz di velt fun ir shmuts erhoybn;
Am   Em   D7   G
Ales opforn vos undz iz lib.
Em   B7
Kemfn tsuzamen vi mechtike laybn
   Am   Em   B7   Em
Far frayhayt, far glaychayt, far undzere printsip.
   C   D7   G   Am
Nit eyn mol hobn shoyn nabele froyen
    D   D7   G
Gemacht tsitern henker un tron;
    B7   Em   D7
Zey hobn getsaygt az men ken zey fertroyen
   G   Am   B7   Em
In bitersten shturm di heylike fon.

Em   B7
Dermont zich an ayere Rushishe shvester,
  Am   Em   D7   G
Dermordet far frahayt fun tsar, dem vampir.
Em   B7
Fermatert biz toyt in di shteynerne nester,
  Am   Em   B7 Em
Fergrobn in shney in dem vistn Sibir.
    C   D7   G   Am
Gedeynkt ir zey? Dan zol zeyer lebn
   D   D7   G
Begaystern aych! Ir zolt mit erfolg
 B7   Em   D7
Lernen un denken, kemfn un shtrebn
    G   Am   B7   Em
Tsu frayhayt un glik far dem arbeter folk.

Em   B7
Help us to lift the world from oppression,
Am   Em   D7   G
Raising up everything that we hold dear.
Em   B7
Struggle together like powerful lions,
   Am   Em   B7   Em
For freedom, equality—principles clear.
   C   D7   G   Am
More than once women have shown that they're able,
    D   D7   G
Made tremble hangman and throne.
    B7   Em   D7
They have shown the world that they can be entrusted
   G   Am   B7   Em
The holy banner in bitterest storm.

Em   B7
Always remember your Russian sisters,
Am   Em   D7   G
Murdered for freedom by bloodsucking tsar.
Em   B7
Slaving to death in stony cold hovels
   Am   Em   B7 Em
And buried in snow in Siberia.
    C   D7   G   Am
Remember them, for their lives are a symbol.
    D   D7   G
Success will be yours—you will break the cruel yoke
   B7   Em   D7
By learning and thinking and fighting and striving
   G   Am   B7   Em
For freedom and joy for all working folk.

As we come marching, marching, unnumbered women dead
Go crying through our singing their ancient song of bread.
Small art and love and beauty their drudging spirits knew.
Yes, it is bread that we fight for,
But we fight for roses, too.

As we come marching, marching, we bring the Greater Days,
The rising of the women means the rising of the race.
No more the drudge and idler, ten that toil where one reposes,
But a sharing of life's glories,
Bread and Roses, Bread and Roses.

—From the poem *Bread and Roses* by
James Oppenheim, inspired by the great
textile workers' strike of Lawrence,
Massachusetts in 1912.

"Free Tom Mooney." May Day parade in the early 1930s.

A BRIV FUN AMERIKE
A LETTER FROM AMERICA

"I am a greenhorn, being only five months out of Odessa, and I cannot forgive myself for being in America now. My head and heart ache when I read in your paper that thousands of workers stand on the barricades in Russia and fight like lions . . . oh, how I would like to be there in the midst of battle, to stand shoulder to shoulder with my comrades that my blood, too, may make our flag red. But the great ocean does not permit one to flee without a ticket, and the boat and railroad do not want to know of my thoughts, and they say that without the dollars they will not take me. Money to pay I have not. What shall I do?"

—From a letter to the editor of the *Jewish Forward* by Joseph Thest, January 20, 1906

By **MARK WARSHAWSKY**

Tay - e - re ma - me, tay - e - re mu - ter, Du __ mayn tay - er
Dear - est Ma - ma, dear - est Moth - er, My __ dear heart, let

ko - sher __ harts, Tsu veys - tu vi ich veyn a - zoy bi - ter,
me __ ex - plain. Do you __ know why I cry __ so bit - ter,

Un __ vi __ tif iz do mayn shmerts? Vos __ volt ich __ nit a
And __ the __ depth of all my pain? I'd __ be all __ my __

vek __ ge - ge - bn Ich __ zol tun oyf dir a blik Ich
rich - es giv - ing, If __ I could see you a - new. For

volt __ far dir ge - shtrekt __ dos le - bn, Ich __ zol ku - men tsu dir tsu - rik.
you __ I'd glad - ly give __ up liv - ing, If __ I __ could but come back to you.

IN KAMF
IN STRUGGLE

In 1876 the Russian poet G. A. Machtet (1852–1901) wrote a poem entitled "Tortured to Death in Captivity," dedicated to martyred student revolutionaries of the 1870s. It was set to a melody of unknown origin and became a traditional song of mourning among Russian revolutionaries. David Edelstadt, who wrote *In Kamf* in 1889, certainly knew the Russian song, and found that his poem was admirably complemented by that melody. *In Kamf* was soon elevated to the status of a quasi-official hymn of Jewish workers all over the world. It enjoyed such popularity and was sung with such fervor at workers' meetings and demonstrations, that Morris Rosenfeld called it the Jewish "Marseillaise."

By **DAVID EDELSTADT**

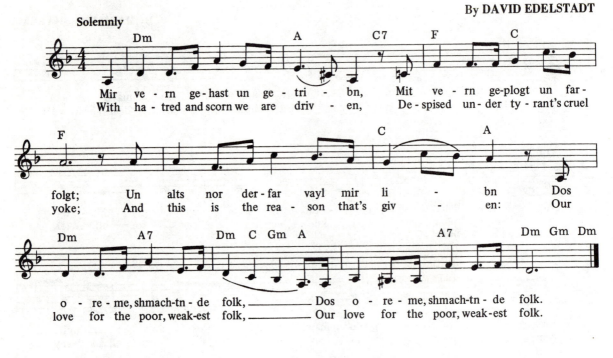

Mir ve-rn ge-hast un ge-tri – bn, Mit ve-rn ge-plogt un far-
With ha-tred and scorn we are driv – en, De-spised un-der ty-rant's cruel

folgt; Un alts nor der-far vayl mir li – bn Dos
yoke; And this is the rea-son that's giv – en: Our

o – re-me, shmach-tn – de folk, _____ Dos o – re-me, shmach-tn – de folk.
love for the poor, weak-est folk, _____ Our love for the poor, weak-est folk.

Dm   A   C7
Mir vern dershosn, gehangen,
F   C   F
Men roybt undz dos lebn un recht;
C A
Derfar vayl mir emes farlangen
Dm   A7   Dm C Gm A
Un frayhayt far oreme knecht,
A7   Dm Gm Dm
Un frayhayt far oreme knecht.

Dm   A   C7
By gun and by rope and by fire
F   C   F
They steal our rights and our lives;
C A
Because of our one true desire:
Dm   A7   Dm C Gm A
Freedom for poor working slaves,
A7   Dm Gm Dm
Freedom for poor working slaves.

176

Dm   A   C7
Shmidt undz in ayzerne keytn,
  F   C   F
Vi blutike chayes undz rayst;
                C A
Ir kent undzer kerper nor teytn
  Dm   A7   Dm C Gm A
Nor keyn mol undzer heylikn gayst.
            A7   Dm Gm Dm
Nor keyn mol undzer heylikn gayst.

   Dm   A   C7
Ir kent undz dermordn, tiranen,
    F   C   F
Naye kemfer vet brengen di tsayt;
               C A
Un mir kemfn, mir kemfn biz vanen
  Dm   A7   Dm C Gm A
Di gantse velt vet vern bafrayt.
        A7   Dm Gm Dm
Di gantse velt vet vern bafrayt.

Dm   A   C7
Cast us in cold iron shackles,
  F   C   F
Like beasts to destroy us you try.
               C A
It's only our bodies you're killing,
  Dm   A7   Dm C Gm A
But our spirit never will die,
        A7   Dm Gm Dm
But our spirit never will die.

   Dm   A   C7
You tyrants can try to destroy us;
    F   C   F
New soldiers will answer the call.
             C A
To battle, to battle till that day
  Dm   A7   Dm C Gm A
When we have brought freedom to all,
        A7   Dm Gm Dm
When we have brought freedom to all.

VOS VET ZAYN DER SOF?
WHAT WILL BE THE END?

"Our craftsmen work not like Christians or Jews, but like heathens, seven days a week; and if they don't work more, it is simply because there are no days left. Still they manage to work nine days in the week by working twelve, fifteen, and, in some instances twenty hours out of twenty-four." (Strike statement by the Central Union of Capmakers, February 1874.) Labor unrest spread from the sweatshops of New York to the sweatshops of Chicago where Isaac Reingold worked. The infamous Haymarket Riot and the subsequent trials and execution of a number of labor leaders in 1886 deeply marked young Isaac. This song grew out of those experiences.

By ISAAC REINGOLD
(1873-1903)

O, e - ln - der ar - bets - man, Shvayg - za - mer knecht, Vos
O, you lone - ly work - ing - man, You si - lent slave, What

hoybt men on mit dir tsu ton? _____ Men roybt dir dayn fray-hayt, Men
can be done to wak - en you? _____ They rob you of free-dom, They

roybt dir dayn recht, Un du nemst dayn kriv - de nit on. _____ Men _
rob you of rights, And yet there is noth - ing you do. _____ They _

lebt oyf dayn chesh - bn, Men ligt oyf dayn kark, Un alts vos du
live off your la - bor, They lie on your neck, And all that you

machst un du tsaygst, _____ Brengt ayn mil - yo - nen Far - me - gn der
make and you show, _____ Earns count - less mil - lions For oth - ers each

mark, Un du shteyst fun vay - tn un shvaygst. _ O, troy - men - de
day, And you si - lent - ly let it be so. _ O, you dream - ing

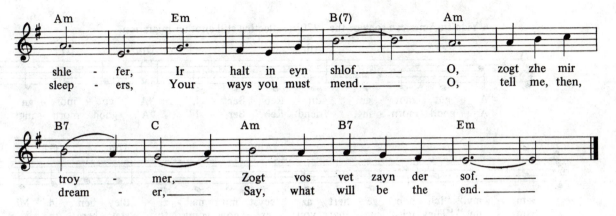

shle - fer,   Ir   halt in eyn shlof._____   O,   zogt zhe mir
sleep - ers,   Your ways you must mend._____   O,   tell me, then,

troy - mer,_____   Zogt vos 'vet zayn der sof. _____
dream - er,_____   Say, what will be the end. _____

Em
Du akerst di felder
    B7   Em
Du zeyst un du shnaydst;
Bm   F♯7   Bm
Di erd shaft a raychn profit!
D7   G
Doch gib a kuk elnder,
B7   Em
Ze vi du laydst;
    Am   D7   G
Dayn feld hot far dir nit geblit.
    Em
Du shpinst oys vol—
            Am
Doch hostu kayn kleyd;
    Em   B(7)
Du hungerst, chotsh du bakst broyt;
    Am
Du shafst nor far yenem
D7   G
A lebn fun freyd;
    Am   B7   Em
Far zich, nor a langzamen toyt! *Chorus*

Em
You plow in the fields,
    B7   Em
And you sow and you reap
Bm   F♯7   Bm
The priceless reward of the land.
D7   G
Just take a look, lonely man,
B7   Em
See your sad fate:
    Am   D7   G
How barren your fields always stand.
    Em
From spinning your wool
            Am
You still have no clothes,
    Em   B(7)
You hunger though you bake the bread.
    Am
You earn a fine living
D7   G
For others, God knows—
    Am   B7   Em
For you, just a slow, endless death. *Chorus*

TO GEY ZICH LERNEN TANTSN
JUST GO AND LEARN TO DANCE NOW

A Yiddish-American song of the 1970's, reflecting still another migration.

"A gut mor - gn, dir, Reb Ber - l," "A gut mor - gn
"A good morn - ing, friend, Reb Ber - l," "A good morn - ing

Sam - my." "Ich hob ge - hert az geyst mit ma - zl Bley - ben in Mi -
Sam - my." "They tell me that you are now going to stay here in Mi -

a - mi. Trogst oyf sich koym zi - bn tsen - dlik Yo - re - lach in
a - mi. Though you're push - ing sev - en - ty, you have - n't lost the

gan - tsn; Heybst du on a tsvey - te yu - gend, To gey zich ler - nen tan - tsn."
chance now, To be - gin a sec - ond child - hood, Just go and learn to dance now."

Chorus

Tra la la la la la la, la la la, la la la.

Tra la la la la la la, la la la, la la la la.

180

```
        C                    Am
Vakst sich shmaltsik di osobe,
      Dm      G7    C
Es vakst on kvelt di talye,
            Am
On dos kleyne klapmashindl
Dm     G7     C
Iz sheyn etvas kalye.

              Am
     Nor der chayshik iz faran,
     Dm    G7      C
   On di oygen glantsn.

                Am
     Heybst du an a tsveyten yugend,
        Dm       G7     C
   To gey zich lernen tantsn. Chorus


        C                 Am
Plonterst zich in karohodl?
      Dm       G7       C
Trachst nit fun keyn yorn.

            Am
Heybst du on a tsveyte yugend,
      Dm    G7    C
Glaych vi naygeborn.

                Am
     Az du bist shoyn a ben shabim,
     Dm     G7    C
   Dos farges in gantsn.

                Am
     Heybst du an a tsveyte yugend,
        Dm       G7     C
   To gey zich lernen tantsn. Chorus
```

```
        C                 Am
Putting on a little weight now,
      Dm      G7     C
And your waist is spreading,
                  Am
And your ticker's working harder—
Dm        G7              C
Who knows where you're heading!

                Am
     But you are as strong as ever,
        Dm       G7    C
   Bright, your eyes are glancing.

                  Am
     To begin a second childhood,
     Dm     G7    C
   Go and take up dancing. Chorus


        C                 Am
Struggle through a circle dance,
      Dm       G7       C
Awkward though you may be,
                  Am
You'll begin a second childhood,
      Dm    G7     C
Like a newborn baby.

                    Am
     Three-score-ten you'll soon be turning,
     Dm     G7    C
   Life is still entrancing.

                  Am
     To begin a second childhood,
     Dm     G7    C
   Go and take up dancing. Chorus
```

The Holocaust

Vilna under Nazi occupation, 1943. Sign in German tells the hours of showing of a Polish film, *The Accursed. (Courtesy Rabbi J.X. Cohen)*

ES BRENT
ON FIRE

Born in Krakow, Poland in 1877, Mordechai Gebirtig wrote poems and songs mirroring the life of the Jewish people around him. With the German invasion of Poland in 1939, that life turned into a horrible nightmare. Gebirtig himself fell victim to the Gestapo during a round-up of Jews in Krakow in 1942.

By **MORDECHAI GEBIRTIG**

Es brent bri - der -lech, es brent!___ Oy, und - zer o - rem shte - tl, ne - bech,
On fire, broth-ers it's on fire! ___ Oh, our poor lit - tle vil - lage is on

brent! ___ Bey - ze vin - tn mit yir - go - zn Ray - sn, bre - chn un tse - blo - zn,
fire! ___ An - gry winds are roar - ing, blow - ing. Tear - ing, break-ing and de-stroy - ing,

Shtar - ker noch di vil - de fla - men, Alts a - rum shoyn brent!
Strong - er still the flames are grow - ing, Ev - 'ry - thing's on fire!

Chorus

Un ir shteyt un kukt a - zoy zich Mit far - leyg - te hent,
And you help - less - ly are watch - ing As the___ flames go higher,

Un ir shteyt un kukt a - zoy zich; Und - zer shte - tl brent!
And you help - less - ly are watch-ing; O - ur town's on fire!

```
    Em    B7          Em
Es brent, briderlech, es brent!
      Am          B7          Em
Oy, undzer orem shtetl, nebech, brent!
    C          Em
S'hobn shoyn di fayer-tsungen,
        Am
Dos gantse shtetl ayngeshlungen—
B7          Em
Un di beyze vintn hudzhen,
      C    D7    G
S'gantse shtetl brent. Chorus
```

```
    Em    B7          Em
Es brent, briderlech, es brent!
      Am          B7          Em
Oy, es ken cholile kumen der moment!
    C          Em
Undzer shtot mit undz tsuzamen
Am
Zol oyf ash avec in flamen,
B7          Em
Blaybn zol—vi noch a shlacht,
        C    D7    G
Nor puste, shvartse vent! Chorus
```

```
    Em    B7          Em
Es brent, briderlech, es brent!
      Am          B7          Em
Di hilf iz nor in aych aleyn gevent!
    C          Em
Oyb dos shtetl iz aych tayer,
  Am
Nemt di keylim, lesht dos fayer.
B7          Em
Lesht mit ayer eygn blut,
      C    D7    G
Bavayzt az ir dos kent!
```

Final chorus

```
    E7          Am
Shteyt nit, brider, ot azoy zich,
Em    Am    B7
Mit farleygte hent.
    Am          Em
Shteyt nit, brider, lesht dos fayer—
A#dim B7  Em
Undzer shtetl brent!
```

```
    Em    B7          Em
On fire, brothers, it's on fire!
      Am          B7          Em
Oh, our poor little village is on fire!
    C          Em
Tongues of flame are wildly leaping,
        Am
Through our town the flames are sweeping,
B7          Em
And the cruel winds keep it burning,
      C    D7    G
The whole town's on fire. Chorus
```

```
    Em    B7          Em
On fire, brothers, it's on fire!
      Am      B7              Em
Oh, God forbid, that it could transpire—
    C          Em
Our town and population,
Am
Victims of an immolation,
B7          Em
Leaving here—like after battle,
      C    D7    G
Blackened walls and mire! Chorus
```

```
    Em    B7          Em
On fire, brothers, it's on fire!
    Am        B7          Em
Only we can stop this awful pyre!
C          Em
If the town is dear to you,
  Am
You'll have to make buckets do.
B7          Em
Put it out with your own blood,
      C    D7    G
Courage you'll acquire.
```

Final chorus

```
    E7          Am
And don't helplessly stand watching
Em    Am    B7
As the flames go higher.
    Am          Em
We must quench the blaze, my brothers—
A#dim B7    Em
Our town's on fire!
```

UNTER DI CHURVES FUN POYLN
UNDER THE RUINS OF POLAND

Words by **ITSIK MANGER**
Music by **S. BERESOVSKY**

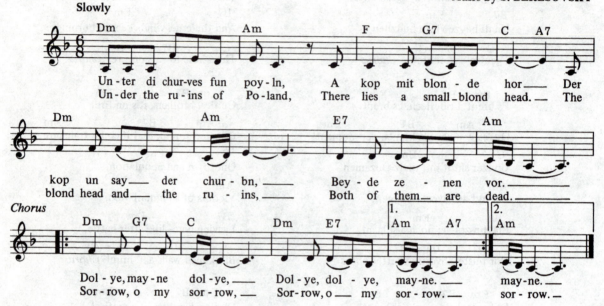

Slowly

Un - ter di chur-ves fun poy-ln, A kop mit blon - de hor____ Der
Un - der the ru - ins of Po-land, There lies a small__blond head.__ The

kop un say__ der chur - bn, ____ Bey - de ze - nen vor._____
blond head and__ the ru - ins, ____ Both of them__ are dead._____

Chorus

Dol - ye, may - ne dol - ye, ____ Dol - ye, dol - ye, may - ne. ____ may - ne. ____
Sor - row, o my sor - row, ____ Sor - row, o my sor - row. ____ sor - row. ____

Dm	Am
Iber di churves fun polyn	Over the ruins of Poland

F G7 C A7	F G7 C A7
Falt un falt der shney,	Falls and falls the snow.

Dm Am	Dm Am
Der blonder kop fun mayn meydl	The blond head of my daughter

E7 Am	E7 Am
Tut mir mesukn vey. *Chorus*	Brings me terrible woe. *Chorus*

Dm Am	Dm Am
Der veytik zitst baym shraybtish	The pain sits at my table,

F G7 C A7	F G7 C A7
Un shraybt a langn briv,	And writes an endless tale.

Dm Am	Dm Am
Di trer in zayne oygn,	The tears that it is shedding,

E7 Am	E7 Am
Iz emesdik un tif. *Chorus*	They are profound and real. *Chorus*

Dm   Am
Iber di churves fun poyln

F   G7   C A7
Flatert a foygl um

Dm   Am
A groyser shive-foygl,

E7   Am
Er tsitert mit di filgl frum. *Chorus*

Dm   Am
Der groyser shive-foygl

F   G7   C A7
(Mayn dershlogn gemit),

Dm   Am
Er trogt oyf zayne fligl

E7   Am
Dos dozike troyer-lid. *Chorus*

Dm   Am
Over the ruins of Poland

F   G7   C A7
A fluttering bird is there.

Dm   Am
The bird is deep in mourning,

E7   Am
It trembles in the air. *Chorus*

Dm   Am
And that great bird of mourning

F   G7   C A7
(O, my soul, how long!),

Dm   A7
Upon its wings it carries

E7   Am
This very mourning song. *Chorus*

ITSIK VITNBERG

Itsik Vitnberg, a shoemaker from Vilna, became a leader of the United Partisan Organization. Plans to defend the ghetto were being made when, on July 15, 1943, Vitnberg was arrested by the Germans. Amazingly, he was rescued by his comrades—but the Nazis did not let matters rest there. An ultimatum was delivered: give up Vitnberg or face immediate and terrible destruction of the ghetto and everyone in it. After much agonizing, Vitnberg bid his comrades farewell and went to his doom. By the end of September the Vilna ghetto itself was no more.

By S. **KACHERGINSKY**

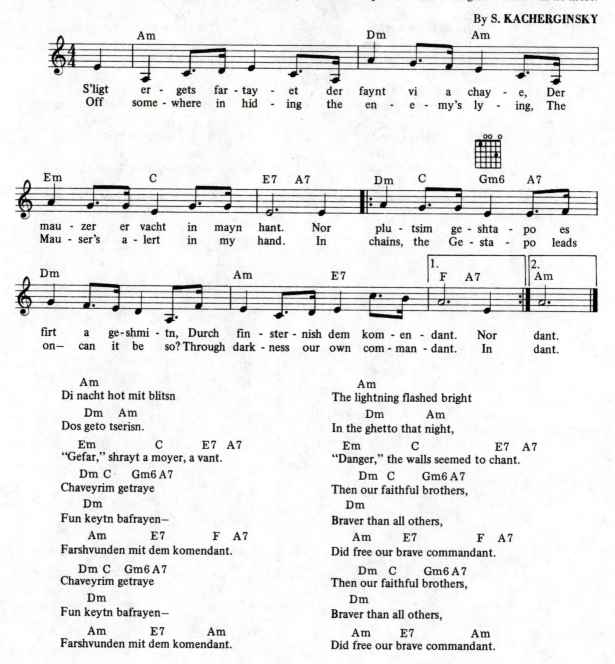

S'ligt er-gets far-tay-et der faynt vi a chay-e, Der
Off some-where in hid-ing the en-e-my's ly-ing, The

mau-zer er vacht in mayn hant. Nor plu-tsim ge-shta-po es
Mau-ser's a-lert in my hand. In chains, the Ge-sta-po leads

firt a ge-shmi-tn, Durch fin-ster-nish dem kom-en-dant. Nor dant.
on— can it be so? Through dark-ness our own com-man-dant. In dant.

Am
Di nacht hot mit blitsn
　Dm　Am
Dos geto tserisn.
　Em　　　C　　E7 A7
"Gefar," shrayt a moyer, a vant.
　Dm C　Gm6 A7
Chaveyrim getraye
　Dm
Fun keytn bafrayen—
　Am　　　E7　　　F A7
Farshvunden mit dem komendant.

　Dm C　Gm6 A7
Chaveyrim getraye
　Dm
Fun keytn bafrayen—
　Am　　　E7　　Am
Farshvunden mit dem komendant.

Am
The lightning flashed bright
　Dm　　　Am
In the ghetto that night,
　Em　　　C　　　　E7 A7
"Danger," the walls seemed to chant.
　Dm C　Gm6 A7
Then our faithful brothers,
　Dm
Braver than all others,
　Am　　E7　　　　F A7
Did free our brave commandant.

　Dm C　Gm6 A7
Then our faithful brothers,
　Dm
Braver than all others,
　Am　　E7　　　Am
Did free our brave commandant.

Am
Di nacht is farfloygn,

   Dm   Am
Der toyt far di oygn,

  Em   C   E7 A7
Di geto, zi fibert in brand.

 Dm C Gm6 A7
In umru di geto,

  Dm
Es drot di geshtapo:

 Am   E7   F A7
"Toyt—oder dem komendant!"

 Dm C Gm6 A7
In umru di geto,

   Dm
Es drot di geshtapo:

 Am   E7   Am
"Toyt—oder dem komendant!"

    Am
Gezogt hot dan Itsik—

  Dm   Am
Un durch vi a blits iz—

   Em   C   E7 A7
"Ich vil nit ir zolt tsulib mir

Dm C Gm6 A7
Darfn dem soyne

  Dm
Dos lebn opgebn. . ."

   Am   E7   F A7
Tsum toyt geyt shtolts der komandir.

 Dm C Gm6 A7
"Darfn dem soyne

  Dm
Dos lebn opgebn. . ."

  Am   E7   Am
Tsum toyt geyt shtolts der komandir.

    Am
Ligt vider fartayet

  Dm   Am
Der faynt vi a chaye,

    Em   C   E7 A7
Mayn mauzer er vacht in mayn hant.

 Dm C Gm6 A7
Itst bistu mir tayer,

  Dm
Zay du mayn befrayer,

 Am   E7   F A7
Zay du itst mayn komendant!

  DmC Gm6 A7
Itst bistu mir tayer,

  Dm
Zay du mayn befrayer,

 Am E7   Am
Zay du itst mayn komendant!

Am
The night, it has ended,

   Dm   Am
And death has descended,

  Em   C   E7 A7
The ghetto in fever does pant.

 Dm C Gm6 A7
For now the Gestapo

   Dm
Threatens all of the ghetto:

     Am   E7   F   A7
"Either death—or give us the commandant."

 Dm C Gm6 A7
For now the Gestapo

   Dm
Threatens all of the ghetto:

     Am   E7   Am
"Either death—or give us the commandant."

     Am
Then Itsik spoke to us

   Dm   Am
With words that went through us:

  Em   C   E7 A7
"To sacrifice you I just can't.

  Dm C Gm6
The cruel enemy

 A7 Dm
Will kill you for me. . ."

    Am   E7   F A7
To death proudly went the commandant.

   Dm C Gm6
"The cruel enemy

 A7 Dm
Will kill you for me. . ."

   Am   E7   Am
To death proudly went the commandant.

  Am
Again, off in hiding,

   Dm   Am
The enemy's lying.

    Em   C   E7 A7
My Mauser's alert in my hand.

  Dm C Gm6 A7
Your value is greater,

   Dm
Be my liberator,

   Am   E7   F A7
For now you are my commandant.

   Dm C Gm6 A7
Your value is greater,

   Dm
Be my liberator,

   Am   E7   Am
For now you are my commandant.

AROYS IZ IN VILNE A NAYER BAFEL
IN VILNA WAS ISSUED A BRAND-NEW DECREE

In April 1943 the Gestapo rounded up the last four thousand Jews of the province of Vilna, Lithuania, from the towns of Oshmene, Soler, Tal, Sventsian, Vidz, and others and brought them to the city of Vilna. From there they were supposed to be transferred to the Kovno ghetto, but this was only a pretext--the closed cattle cars in which the people were being transported went only as far as the nearby town of Ponar. At that point the slaughter began and the Jews realized their deception too late. Nevertheless, many of them desperately attacked their guards with fists, clubs, and even teeth. Several Germans were killed in the melee. About thirty Jews escaped.

A - roys iz in Vil - ne a nay - er ba - fel, Tsu
In Vil - na was is - sued a brand - new de - cree, To

bren - gn di yid - n fun shtet - lech, ____ Ge - bracht hot men a - le fun
sum - mon all Jews we were bid - den. ____ They gath - ered to - geth - er the

yun - ge biz alt, A - fi - le oych kran - ke oyf bet - lech. ____
young and the old, And e - ven the sick and bed - rid - den. ____

G
Tsunoyfgeshpart hot men dem lager,
  D7   G B7
Men hot zey genumen sortirn:
Em   Am
Oshmene yidn in Vilne tsu blaybn,
  Em B7   Em
Un Soler in Kovne tsu firn.

   G
Aroysgefirt hot men fun lager,
D7   G B7
Yunge un frishe korbones.
Em   Am
Arayngeshpart hot men zey alemen glaych
  Em B7 Em
In di zelbe farmachte vagones.

G
The camp became crowded with thousands of Jews,
  D7   G B7
And then they began the selection:
Em   Am
Jews from Oshemene in Vilna would stay,
   Em B7   Em
Send Solers in Kovno's direction.

   G
The first group of martyrs was led from the camp.
  D7   G B7
"More victims!" the order was worded.
Em   Am
Then jammed all together like animals,
  Em B7   Em
They into the sealed boxcars were herded.

G
Der tsug iz sich langsam geforn,
  D7   G B7
Gefayft un gegebn sirenes.

 Em   Am
Stantsie Ponar—der tsug shtelt zich op,

   Em   B7   Em
Men tshepet dort op di vagones.

G
Zey hobn derzen az men hot zey farfirt,
  D7   G B7
Men firt tsu der shreklicher sh'chite.

   Em   Am
Zey hobn tsebrochn di tir fun vagon,

   Em B7   Em
Genumen aleyn machn pleyte.

G
Zey hobn gevorfn zich af der geshtapo,
D7   G B7
Un zey di kleyder tserisn.

  Em   Am
Geblibn zaynen lign lebn di yidn,

  Em B7   Em
Etleche daytshn tsebisn.

G
S'hobn di getos fun der provints,
  D7   G B7
Gegebn fir toyznt korbones.

  Em   Am
Un opgefirt hot men di zachn fun zey,

  Em   B7   Em
Tsurik in di zelbe vagones,

G
Then slowly the train made its way down the tracks,
  D7   G B7
The whistles and sirens were blowing.

  Em   Am
But when it reached Ponar it came to a halt,

  Em   B7   Em
And then the uncoupling got going.

G
They realized then that they had been betrayed,
     D7   G B7
And that they would be killed at the station.

   Em   Am
So, smashing the door to the box car,

      Em   B7   Em
They all tried escaping in great desperation.

G
They threw themselves bodily on the Gestapo,
 D7   G B7
Biting and clawing and crying;

 Em   Am
And next to the bodies of Jews on the ground,

Em B7   Em
Several Germans were lying.

G
From ghettos of all of the province around,
   D7   G B7
Some four thousand martyrs were given,

 Em   Am
And all their belongings were shipped back again

   Em   B7   Em
In the same cars in which they'd been driven.

Jews arriving from outlying villages to fill up the Vilna Ghetto, 1943. *(Courtesy Rabbi J.X. Cohen)*

GETO LID
GHETTO SONG

By **LEYB OPESKIN**

Song of the Vilna ghetto.

Far - vos iz der hi - ml ge - ven nech - tn loy - ter, Fun
Oh why was the sky yes - ter - day all un - cloud - ed, With

freyd hot ge - shaynt ye - de gas? Far - vos iz di zun a - za
sun - shine and warmth stream - ing down? And why does the sun, which was

lich - ti - ke roy - te, Far - chmu - ret haynt beyz un in kas? Far -
shin - ing so bright - ly, To - day hide its face with a frown? And

vos iz di zun a - za lich - ti - ke roy - te, Far - chmu - ret haynt beyz un in kas?
why does the sun which was shin - ing so bright - ly, To - day hide its face with a frown?

Am Dm	Am Dm
Es troyert der himl, der hoyf un dos gesl,	For heaven is mourning, and so is our courtyard,
G7 C E7	G7 C E7
Es troyert dos harts shtilerheyt.	In silence our hearts also mourn.
Am Dm	Am Dm
Tsi ken men fargesen, tsi meg men fargesen	How can we forget, yes, how dare we forget,
G7 C E7	G7 C E7
Fargangene shoen fun freyd?	The hours of joy that are gone?
Am A7 Dm	Am A7 Dm
Tsi ken men fargesen, tsi meg men fargesen	How can we forget, yes, how dare we forget,
Am E7 Am	Am E7 Am
Fargangene shoen mit freyd.	The hours of joy that are gone?

Am　　　　　　　Dm
Vish oys dayne oygen, farges dayne zorgn,
　G7　　　　　　C　E7
Tsu troyern iz nit keday.
　　Am　　　　　　Dm
Ken zayn shoyn az morgn, s'meg zayn shoyn

　　az morgn
　G7　　　　　　　C　E7
Vet oyfshaynen zun oyfdosnay.
　　Am　　　　　A7　　　Dm
Ken zayn shoyn az morgn, s'meg zayn shoyn

　　az morgn
　Am　　　E7　　　Am
Vet oyfshaynen zun oyfdosnay.

　　Am　　　　　　　Dm
So dry up your eyes and forget all your sorrow,
　G7　　　　　　　　　C　E7
For mourning is not worth the pain.
　　Am　　　　　　Dm
It can be that soon—it may be

　　tomorrow,
　G7　　　　　　　C　E7
The sun will be shining again.
　　Am　　　A7　　　Dm
It can be that soon—it may be

　　tomorrow,
　Am　　　E7　　　Am
The sun will be shining again.

Jews arriving in the Ghetto from outlying villages of Vilna province, 1943.
(Courtesy Rabbi J.X. Cohen)

YEDER RUFT MICH ZIAMELE
PEOPLE CALL ME ZIAMELE

The children in the ghetto would play and laugh, and in their games the entire tragedy was reflected. They would play at gravedigging: they would dig a pit and would put a child inside and call him Hitler.... And they used to play funerals.

—Dr. Aaron Peretz, a survivor of the Kovno ghetto

Ye - der ruft mich Zia - me - le, Ay, vi mir iz shver.
Peo - ple call me Zia - me - le, Life is hard to bear.

Ch'ob ge - hat a ma - me - le, Ch'ob zi shoyn nit mer.
Once I had a ma - me - le, Now she is no - where.

Ch'ob ge - hat a ta - te - le, Hot er mir ge - hit.
Once I had a fa - ther dear, And a kind one, too.

Itst bin ich a shma - te - le, Vayl ich bin a yid.
Now I shed a bit - ter tear, For I am a Jew.

Am
Ch'ob gehat a shvesterl,

Dm E7 Am
Iz zi mer nishto.

G7 C
Ach, vu biztu, Esterl,

G7 C E7
In der shverer sho?

Am E7 Am
Ergets ba a boymele,

A7 Dm
Ergets ba a ployt,

G7 E7 Am F
Ligt mayn bruder, Shloymele.

Dm E7 Am
Fun a daytsh getoyt.

Am
I did have a sister, too,

Dm E7 Am
Now she is no more.

G7 C
Esther, what's become of you

G7 C E7
In this awful war?

Am E7 Am
Somewhere near a little tree,

A7 Dm
Somewhere on the ground,

G7 E7 Am F
Lies my brother, Shloymele—

Dm E7 Am
Germans shot him down.

194

Am
Ch'ob gehat a heymele,

Dm E7 Am
Itster iz mir shlecht.

G7 C
Ich bin vi a beheymele,

G7 C E7
Vos der talyen shecht.

Am E7 Am
Got, du kuk fun himele,

A7 Dm
Af der erd arop.

G7 E7 Am F
Ze nor vi dayn blimele

Dm E7 Am
Shnaydt der talyen op.

Am
Once I had a little home,

Dm E7 Am
Now the times are hard.

G7 C
Like an animal I roam,

G7 C E7
In the slaughter yard.

Am E7 Am
God, who looks down from the skies,

A7 Dm
Down upon the land,

G7 E7 Am F
Hear the little childrens' cries—

Dm E7 Am
Killed at every hand.

Vilna under Nazi occupation, 1943. *(Courtesy Rabbi J.X. Cohen)*

S'DREMLIN FEYGL
BIRDS ARE DOZING

A ghetto lullaby.

By **LEAH RUDNITZKY**

Slowly

S'drem - lin fey - gl oyf di tzvey - gn, Shlof mayn tay - er - e
On the branch - es birds are doz - ing, Heads be - neath their

kind. Bay___ dayn vi - gl, oyf dayn no - re
wings. Sleep___ my dear___ one, by your cra - dle

Zitst a fremd - e un zingt. Bay — dayn vi - gl, oyf dayn no - re
Sits a strang - er and sings. Sleep — my dear — one, by your cra - dle

Zitst a fremd - e un zingt. Loo — loo, loo — loo loo.
Sits a strang - er and sings.

Em
S'iz dayn vigl vu geshtanen,

G   E7
Oysgeflochten fun glik.

Am   D Am   Em
Un dayn mame, oy, dayn mame,

Am   E7   Am
Kumt shoyn keyn-mol nit tsurik.

    D   Am   Em
Un dayn mame, oy, dayn mame,

Am   Dm   E
Kumt shoyn keyn-mol nit tsurik.

    Am   F E
Loo loo, loo loo loo.

Em
Once upon a time your cradle,

G   E7
It brought joy to all.

Am   D Am   Em
But your mother, oh, your mother—

Am E7   Am
She is gone beyond recall.

        D Am   Em
But your mother, oh, your mother—

Am Dm   E
She is gone beyond recall.

        Am   F E
Loo loo, loo loo loo.

196

Em
Ch'ob gezen dayn taten loyfn,

  G   E7
Unter hogel fun shteyn.

Am D Am Em
Iber felder iz gefloygen

 Am   E7   Am
Zayn far-yosemter geveyn.

   D Am Em
Iber felder iz geflogen

Am Dm   E
Zayn far-yosemter geveyn.

    Am   F E
  Loo loo, loo loo loo.

Em
I have seen your father running,

  G   E7
Stones falling like hail.

 Am   D   Am Em
And came echoing over meadows,

Am   E7   Am
His long-suffering wail.

        D Am Em
And came echoing over meadows,

Am Dm   E
His long-suffering wail.

    Am   F E
  Loo loo, loo loo loo.

YUGNT-HIMN
YOUTH HYMN

The very expression of apathy indicates submission to the enemy, which can cause our collapse morally and root out of our hearts our hatred for the invader. It can destroy within us the will to fight; it can undermine our resolution. . . . Our young people must walk with heads erect.

—From the *Voice of Youth*, an underground
publication of the Vilna ghetto

Words by **SH. KACHERGINSKY**
Music by **BASYA RUBIN**

G
Ver es voglt um oyf vegn,

    Am   D7   G D7
Ver mit draystkayt s'shtelt zayn fus,

    G   E7
Brengt di yugnt zey antkegn,

    A7 D7 G
Funem geto a gerus. *Chorus*

G
He who sets forth on the highway,

    Am   D7   G D7
And with boldness strikes the fore,

    G   E7
Let him come and travel my way,

    A7 D7 G
Greetings from us all will flow. *Chorus*

```
         G
Mir gedenken ale sonim,
      Am   D7   G    D7
Mir gedenken ale fraynt.
      G                   E7
Eybig veln mir dermonen,
      A7  D7      G
Undzer nechtn mitn havnt. *Chorus*


         G
Kloybn mir tsunoyf di glider,
      Am D7      G   D7
Vider shteln mir di rey.
      G                   E7
Geyt a boyer, geyt a shmider,
      A7 D7      G
Lomir ale geyn mit zey. *Chorus*
```

```
         G
When our enemies oppress us,
      Am   D7    G    D7
We remember our friends.
      G                    E7
And our foes cannot distress us,
      A7  D7          G
For the darkest night soon ends. *Chorus*


         G
We will gather all together,
      Am   D7       G    D7
Once again we'll form our ranks.
      G                       E7
Workers, march through stormy weather,
      A7D7       G
You will earn eternal thanks. *Chorus*
```

Israel Maizelis (author's mother's cousin) in his Red Army uniform, 1945.

NEYN, NEYN, NEYN
NO, NO, NO

SHTIL, DI NACHT
STILL, THE NIGHT

Jewish partisan song of the Vilna uprising against the Nazi army in 1943.

By **HIRSH GLIK**

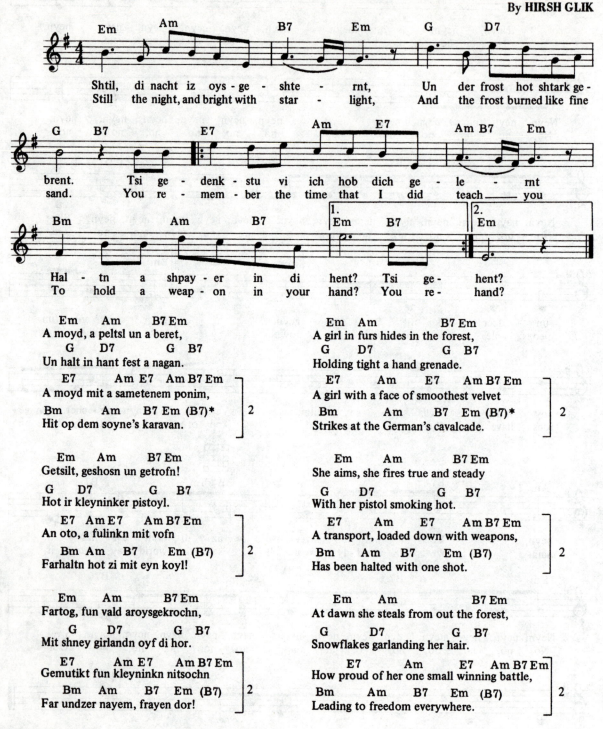

Shtil, di nacht iz oys-ge-shte-rnt, Un der frost hot shtark ge-
Still, the night, and bright with star-light, And the frost burned like fine

brent. Tsi ge-denk-stu vi ich hob dich ge-le-rnt
sand. You re-mem-ber the time that I did teach you

Hal-tn a shpay-er in di hent? Tsi ge-hent?
To hold a weap-on in your hand? You re-hand?

Em   Am   B7 Em
A moyd, a peltsl un a beret,
G   D7   G B7
Un halt in hant fest a nagan.
E7   Am E7   Am B7 Em
A moyd mit a sametenem ponim,
Bm   Am   B7 Em (B7)*
Hit op dem soyne's karavan.   2

Em   Am   B7 Em
Getsilt, geshosn un getrofn!
G   D7   G B7
Hot ir kleyninker pistoyl.
E7   Am E7   Am B7 Em
An oto, a fulinkn mit vofn
Bm Am B7   Em (B7)
Farhaltn hot zi mit eyn koyl!   2

Em   Am   B7 Em
Fartog, fun vald aroysgekrochn,
G   D7   G B7
Mit shney girlandn oyf di hor.
E7   Am E7   Am B7 Em
Gemutikt fun kleyninkn nitsochn
Bm   Am   B7 Em (B7)
Far undzer nayem, frayen dor!   2

Em   Am   B7 Em
A girl in furs hides in the forest,
G   D7   G B7
Holding tight a hand grenade.
E7   Am   E7   Am B7 Em
A girl with a face of smoothest velvet
Bm   Am   B7 Em (B7)*
Strikes at the German's cavalcade.   2

Em   Am   B7 Em
She aims, she fires true and steady
G   D7   G B7
With her pistol smoking hot.
E7   Am   E7   Am B7 Em
A transport, loaded down with weapons,
Bm   Am   B7   Em (B7)
Has been halted with one shot.   2

Em   Am   B7 Em
At dawn she steals from out the forest,
G   D7   G B7
Snowflakes garlanding her hair.
E7   Am   E7   Am B7 Em
How proud of her one small winning battle,
Bm   Am   B7   Em (B7)
Leading to freedom everywhere.   2

*B7: for repeats.

ZOG NIT KEYNMOL
NEVER SAY

   When the April 1943 round up of Jews began, the Vilna-born poet Hirsh Glik escaped and joined the Partisans. It was the time of the heroic uprising in the Warsaw ghetto and Glik was inspired to write this song. It soon became the official hymn of the Jewish Partisans. With the liquidation of the Vilna ghetto, Glik was captured by the Gestapo and sent to a concentration camp in Estonia. When the Red Army swept through the area the following year, he escaped from the camp, only to be killed fighting the Germans in the nearby woods. He was twenty-four.

By **HIRSH GLIK**

Zog nit keyn-mol az-du geyst dem lets-tn veg, Chotsh him-len
Nev-er say that you are on your fi-nal road, Though o-ver-

blay-e-ne far-shte-ln bloy-e teg; Vayl ku-men
head dark skies of lead may death for-bode; The long-a-

vet noch und-zer oys-ge-benkt-te sho, Es vet a
wait-ed ho-ur's sure-ly draw-ing near, When with a

poyk ton und-zer trot: mir zay-nen do! Vayl ku-men do.
roar our steps will thun-der: we are here! The long-a-here!

B7		Em	B7		Em

Fun grinem palmen-land biz vaytn land fun shney, From land of palm tree to the far-off land of snow,

D7 G D7 G
Mir kumen on mit undzer payn, mit undzer vey, Our people come together crushed by pain and woe.

E7 Am E7 Am
Un vu gefaln s'iz a shprits fun undzer blut, But where a drop of our blood has touched the ground,

B7 Em B7 Em
Shprotsn vet dort undzer gvure undzer mut. There our strength and our courage will resound.

B7 Em B7 Em
Dos lid geshriben íz mit blut un nit mit blay, This song is written down with blood and not with lead,

D7 G D7 G
S'iz nit a lidl fun a foygl oyf der fray. The birds don't sing it, for it fills the air with dread.

E7 Am E7 Am
Dos hot a folk ts'vishn falndike vent This song was sung as all around us bullets sprayed,

B7 Em B7 Em
Dos lid gezungen mit naganes in di hent! And walls collapsed as people hurled their hand grenades.

203

ANI MAAMIN
I BELIEVE

Based on the *Thirteen Articles of Faith* by the twelfth-century philosopher Moses Maimonides, this song—sung in the Hebrew—became the hymn of the multitudes swallowed up by the extermination camps.

A - ni ma - a-min, a - ni ma - a-min, A - ni ____ ____ ma - a -
I be - lieve, ____ I be - lieve, ____ I - be - lieve, I be -

min, A - ni ____ ma - a -
lieve, I be - lieve, ____

min, Be - e - mu - nah she - ley - mah,
With a per - fect faith ____ I be - lieve,

Be - e - mu - nah she - ley - mah, Be - vi - at
With a per - fect faith, ___ I be - lieve, In the com - ing

ha - mo - shi - ah, Be - vi - at ha - mo - shi - ah a - ni
of ___ the Mes - si - ah, In Mes - si - ah's com - ing I be -

ma - a - min. Ve - af al pi she - yit - mah - mey - ah
lieve. ____ Al - though he lin - ger, yet I do be - lieve,

Im ____ kol ____ zot ____ a - ni ma - a - min.
E - ven though he lin - ger I be - lieve.

BASIC GUITAR CHORDS

Key to symbols employed in this chart:

P = Primary Bass String
A = Alternate Bass String
x = String Not To Be Played
o = Open String To Be Played
(3) = Finger May Be Moved For Alternate Bass
▬ = Barre

Note: The number immediately to the right of some of the barres indicates the fret at which the barre is placed.

The diagrams of some chords may differ here from the way they were pictured elsewhere in this book. These are alternate fingerings—all are equally correct.

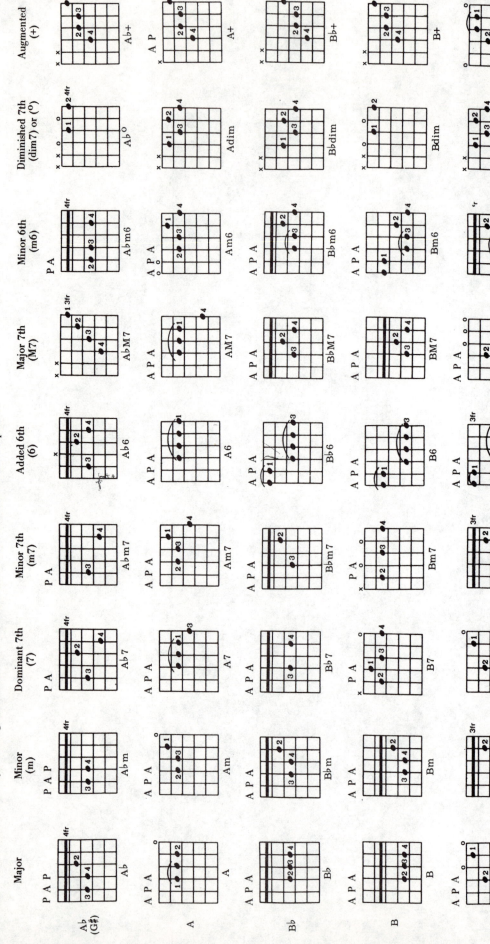

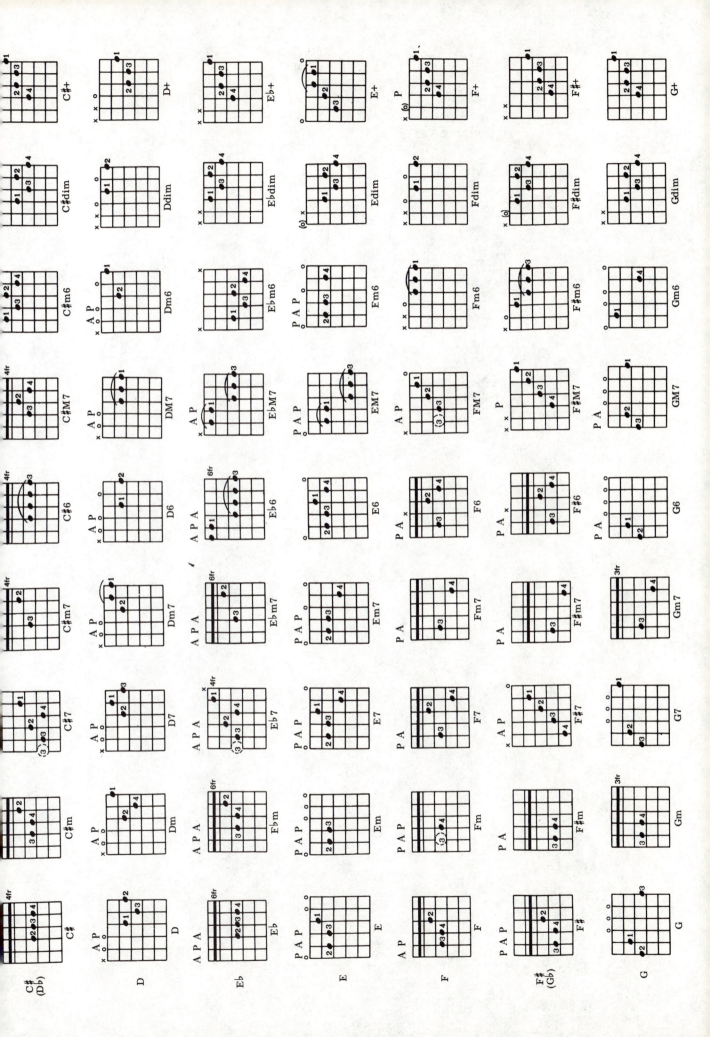